THE WORLD'S MOST BEAUTIFUL PLACES

Text by

JEAN MATHÉ

Crescent Books
New York

End papers : a grandiose lanscape in Kashmir.
Title page : the valley of Ait Bou Guemmez,
in Morocco, shortly before one of the frequent
storms of the month of August.

Designed and produced by
Editions Minerva SA

First English edition published by
Editions Minerva SA

Copyright © 1984 by
Minerva Editions S.A., Genève.

This 1984 edition is published
by Crescent Books.
Distributed by Crown Publishers, Inc.

Printed in Italy

Library of Congress Cataloging
in Publication Data

ISBN: 0-517-463296

INTRODUCTION

Man only appeared very late or, if you prefer it, has only very recently arrived on this earth of ours.

The planet already had an amazing geological and tectonic past by then. It is this that was responsible for the climate, for the relief and so, as a result, for the different landscapes that make up our environment.

It was the depth of life of the magma, the continental drift, and closer to us in our daily lives, erosion by wind and sea and falling rain, that were responsible for the framework of our lives and the panoramas that we seek throughout the world. It should especially not be believed that these geological elements static and inert; far from being fixed and unmoving, the components of geology are in a state of perpetual mutation.

The history of the most beautiful natural sites in the world is thus constantly developing, and nothing is more dynamic than the countryside. Nothing is more logical either, and an explanation of all this sites can be found by a study of physics or chemistry, that is, the causes are basically scientific.

The phenomena of chiselling away and moulding nature are prodigious forces, invisible or spectacular, but they are always determinant, which means that they are themselves sometimes even tourist attractions.

Several of these determinisms of the countryside, for example, are violent or highly scenic: the volcanos, especially those in a state of permanent activity, for the fantastic sight that they offer; the other manifestations of vulcanism— hot water springs, fumeroles, geysers and sometimes earth quakes; the breaks in the earth's crust, such as the African Rift, where one can best see, in a diabolical setting, the confrontation of the tectonic blocks; ice-fields, ice-packs or glaciers, whose crystal world is in a state of perpetual reshaping; the ocean, eternally sculpting the coasts and never ceasing to touch up its work.

Others are more subtle and so discreet that one would never suspect them of wielding such power; the wind which seems to claw at all it touches, especially when loaded with sand; the rain that erodes, and swells the running waters that carve out their course in the earth and hollow out the caves, which they decorate with their fairylike concretions.

And man must not be forgotten, man who forms and transforms the countryside, to meet the needs of his agriculture (irrigation, terracing, crops).

Thus, from a violent physical manifestation, such as an eruption or from the meeting between a drop of water and some crumbly limestone, can spring the charm, the uncanniness, the softness, the elegance or the grossness that can transform part of our planet into a listed site which people flock from all over the world to visit.

Our earth can offer beauties of an extraordinary variety : the sea — which covers two thirds of the planet — tirelessly breaking upon the rocks, as here at the farthest extremity of Brittany (top, left); erosion, which creates veritable natural monuments, as in Monument Valley, in Arizona (above); glaciers which, as they have advanced, have formed numerous lakes, in Norway, for example (left).

THE VALLEY OF CHAMONIX, GAVARNIE THE PUYS D'AUVERGNE

In the heart of the Alps, the humble valley of Chamonix, formed by the course of the river Arve, with its turbulent milky waters, offers the most outstanding synthesis in Europe of high mountain landscapes in their most perfect expression. Nowhere else have the fairylike offshoots of the folds, having rejuvenated the old Hercynian crests to tertiary formations, formed within so small a distance so many spectacular sights, mountain masterpieces in the Alpine world. As if for the setting of a masterly production, all the elements indispensable to the secret and exciting alchemy of the peaks are to be found there: rock, snow and ice; each in turn, come the wind, the mist, the clouds and the sun to cast over them a spell of mysticism, poetry or drama, on a common background of fascinating and grandiose beauty.

Jagged needle-like rocky peaks piercing the sky, with the terrifying yet marvellous stone lacework of the Grépon, contrasting with the solid granite mass of the Verte or the Drus, without doubt the most impressive in the Alps. The magnificent glaciers of Argentière, the Bossons and especially of the sea of ice. Majestic petrified rivers, their movement frozen at the foot of the mountain face; indiscreet tongues,

here that in 1786 and 1787 modern alpinism was born, with the first ascensions of Balmat and Saussine.

How different the Gavarnie Cirque appears. The pearl of the Pyrenees, it has the charm and the refined aestheticism so typical of this range of mountains, less overpowering than that of the Alps. Attracted by their beauty, wild but accessible, the Romantics were captivated by this type of mountain. Hugo, Sand, Vigny, Musset, all came to dream before the rocky tiers, recalling so perfectly the Dantesque hemicycle of a vast theatre, adorned with a slender capricious waterfall. The literary vocation of the setting has crowned it with all that is fantastic and marvellous: the famous "Roland's Breach", a gash cut in the topmost cliff could only be, from then onwards, the scar made by the legendary Durandale during the heroic battle fought against the Saracens by the valiant nephew of Charlemagne.

France. Right : the *Aiguilles du Dru* and *lac des Gaillands*. Below : the rocky steps of the Gavarnie Cirque, the "Pearl of the Pyrenees". Below : the charm of the undulating chain of the Puys of Auvergne (left) and the dramatic look of the Sea of Ice.

rough and stiffly icy, caressing with their silvery kiss the most hidden and the most inhospitably steep mountainsides, such as that of the Jorasses. And, dominating everything around it, the immaculate dome of Mont-Blanc, whose topmost ridge, looking almost unreal as it towers to a height of 4,807 metres, is wreathed in a vaporous mane of snow, ruffled and blown, at the mercy of the wind.

In contrast, how gentle are the slopes of the softer range of the Puys d'Auvergne, stretching its undulating spine out over a distance of about forty kilometres, to the south of Clermont-Ferrand! It has learnt the secret of covering with bucolic pastures the indications of its recent vulcanism. The frothing summits of the broad cones mark out perfect craters, in which there is sometimes a lake set within the girdle of dark firs, like the plantation of Pavin. The landscape, dominated by the rounded back of the Puy de Dôme would look like a moonscape if it was not also green, and disturbing if it was not also pastoral.

It comes as no surprise to know, then, that it was

THE POINTE DU RAZ AND
DE PEN HIR
THE CLIFFS OF ÉTRETAT

The Crozon peninsula is without doubt the wildest and the most tormented of the whole of the Atlantic coast. Its spearhead, the *Pointe de Pen Hir*, is the advanced stronghold in its eternal fight against the sea which pounds upon it mercilessly. Heroic in its hopeless struggle, it is retreating stone by stone, dislodged by the inexorable combination of the erosion of the earth (caused by rain, wind, frost and sun) and the buffeting blows which are constantly being struck against it by the most terrible tides in Europe.

This wearing away of the peninsulas of the "terres finissantes" (Finistère), eaten away and stripped by the all-powerful ocean, finds its most moving illustration, and also the most impressive, in the magnificent *Pointe du Raz*.

A breathtakingly steep path, clinging to the jagged cliffs, runs right round the cape, looking down on abysses and chasms, into which the sea races. The Hell of Plogoff is the most outstanding of tourist sights. A devilish realm of foam and tumult, where the ocean rollers pound the rocks as they break with the dull, moaning sound of someone groaning in pain. Out at sea, the tiny island of Sein, the sacrificed sentry, desolate and treeless, is an irratio-

nal challenge by a piece of land. Just like the rocky plateau of Ouessant, set in the sea off Brest and crowned with a wreath of dangerous-looking rocky peaks, alas tragically famous. A rugged universe, harassed by currents, splashed by furiously foaming spray, a battle-field for the agelong confrontation between the granite and the sea, swept by the fearful gusty blasts of a mad wind.

Nor does the sea ever relax its merciless pounding on the high cliff which runs along the plateau of the land of Caux, between Le Havre and Dieppe. But here, the elegant rampart along the coast, dazzling in its whiteness, has not the same resistance as the Breton granite. And the beautiful chalk walls, attacked just as much by the rain-water running down them as by the tireless battering of the waves of the sea, are retreating in disorder. The high slices of the chalky cake lie in alternation with parallel strata of silex, which make the whole thing look like a huge Genoese pastry. They are falling to pieces, leaving lying along the coast strange masses of pale-looking ruins, with one foot already in the sea which will eventually swallow them up.

France. Above : the high chalky cliff of the area of Caux, at Etretat. Right : the formidable *Pointe du Raz*. Below : the splendours of the Côte d'Azur (at Cap Ferrat).

GRANDE BRIÈRE
THE POITOU MARSHLANDS
LA CAMARGUE

Between the region of the Loire and Brittany, earth and water are still fighting over this tertiary depression, partly filled in with alluvium. Over an area of several thousands of acres spreads the Grande Brière. Fascinating marshland, with its landscapes, muted in colour and in sound, and steeped in the melancholic and poetic nostalgia of the world of water; silent, indeed, but bristling with hidden life. Man is there to see that the canals to drain the marsh and to permit access to the region are kept open and in order. A couple of dozen villages encircle this secret and almost magic realm of reeds. Fédrun, a former "island" emerging from the sleeping waters, and St-Joachim, perched just at the edge of them, are the best starting-points from which to discover this peaceful little world, where herons and dragonflies reign, as well as otters and tenches, amongst the flounces of the water-lilies and the duckweed.

The Poitou marshlands, on the other hand, are one of man's creations. A few centuries ago, there was nothing there but swampy and sterile low-lying land, filling with coastal mud the old gulf of the Pictons, an indentation of the coast stretching as far as Niort. The monks of the abbeys, which were built on the rare high spots emerging from the marshland, began their task of draining the area as early as the 10th century. Henri IV appealed to the Dutch for help (in the 16th century), and gradually a network of canals "dried up" the land, to make it fit for cultivation. But there still remains a small piece of "wet marsh", which runs alongside the river Sèvre from Coulon to Marans. A complicated square pattern of "trenches" and "levees" (acting as dykes), reaches and locks, attempts to mitigate the effect of the stagnation of the waters, the consequence of the fact that the slope of the land is extremely gradual. Yet this "green Venice" is flooded every winter, fertilizing the peaty "chequer-boards", lined with willow stocks, and slender poplars, where cows graze, cows that have to be brought here by boat. In these Dutch-type surroundings one can find all the charm and mystery of a land of water. But here, the usual inhabitants to be found in a watery world (carp, eels, teal and mallards) must share their territory with the farmers, gliding along the canals in their wide black flat-bottomed boats.

With its salty plain and its marshy delta enclosed between the two arms of the Rhone, the Camargue is a well-favoured spot. Hollowed out by the small interior sea of the Vaccarés, and swept by the invigorating blasts of the mistral wind, its luminous landscape is famous throughout the world. Brayer, Giono, Daudet and Mistral have immortalized its hidden lagoons, fringed with reeds, a precious refuge for flamingoes; and its damp pastures where, between the salt pans and the last cowherds' cottages, herds of fighting bulls wander and wild horses gallop.

Left: a small canal lined with willows in the Poitevin Marshes and a view of the famous Galamus gorge. **Right**: the fascinating marsh of the *Grande Brière*. **Opposite**: a view of the Camargue, with the famous wild horses to be found in the region.

THE TARN AND VERDON GORGES
THE GORGE OF GALAMUS

To get away from the buttresses of the Massif Central, the Tarn must, as it flows down Mount Lozère, make a twisting, difficult course for itself, carving deeply into the rocky plateau of the Causses. The result of this is a most impressive mineral section, an ever-changing and tortuously winding corridor of stone, considered to be one of the finest sights in France. As far as Ste-Éminie, the shallow valley opens out wide, by means of sloping dolomitic rock-faces on the uneven surfaces of the Causse Méjean and Sauveterre. Then the river plunges into a canyon which becomes more and more closed in as it narrows. From time to time, the ruins of some forgotten feudal fortress, or the old houses of a medieval village, clustered close together in their fear of attack, and perched on a high peak, add to the impression of desolate solitude in the barren rocks which emanates from this geological scar. Majestic grandeur and serene beauty are indeed the most fitting qualities to attribute to all that one can see as one makes one's way through these magnificent gorges. From time to time, however, an ever-changing variety of scenery softens a little the stark, almost sacred, atmosphere created by some of the rocky cliffs: here and there, the water, rumbling and foaming with rage, is forced to find a way out, heaving to release itself from the imprisoning hold of the cliff wall; elsewhere, the river sparkling with its opalescent highlights, slows down to a gentle meandering pace, to sweep calmly round the wide bends, between two pebbly beaches, at the foot of high rock-faces, their colours ranging from the yellowish-white of the chalky stone, to the deep reddish-yellow of the sandstone. With, here and there, some groves of straggling foliage, or the wavy fronds of overgrown clumps of grass, the only sign of vegetable life to be seen in them.

Without going as far as some enthusiasts have done in comparing this canyon with the Grand Canyon in Colorado, it can, nevertheless, be said that the Verdon canyon, which runs into the Durance, is unique in Europe. Over a distance of some thirteen miles, this magnificent chasm, yawning in the Jurassic limestone of Provence, seems to hide itself away, as if it were ashamed of having been hollowed out by so insignificant a stream of water! From the edge of the plateau, smelling strongly of thyme, garrigue and warm lavender, the view is overpowering and almost oppressive in its great beauty. At the bottom of a whole tumultuous tangle of karstic anticlines, heaped up like huge *millefeuilles,* the bright emerald-green foaming serpent of the torrent threads its way, winding its coils between the breathtakingly steep rock-faces, which can reach up to a height of 700 metres of sheer cliff. Still keeping some hidden recesses, almost unknown and unseen, because of the difficulty of gaining access to them, the Verdon gorge remains one of the spots where sportsmen like to test their strength to its limits. Whether it be in climbing the vertical rock-faces, amongst the most challenging to be found in modern alpinism; or in defying the dangerously wild rapids, following in the footsteps of Martel, who was the first to go through them on a makeshift raft at the beginning of the century.

Beside such world-famous touristic sights, the tiny gorge of Galamus seems out of place. In Roussillon, near Maury, linking the massif of the Corbières with the valley of the Agly, it provides nevertheless, a unique geological attraction. For, even if it is easily the shortest and the shallowest, it can also boast of being the narrowest. An incredible convulsive fault, it looks like a miniature, a model, giving an example of all the elements necessary for an ideal gorge: in less than one kilometre, a seemingly impossible road runs right through it along a kind of ledge, where it is only possible to pass where there are narrow lay-bys, arranged in the hollow of bends which appear every ten metres like little resting-places. The views to be had from this breathtaking tectonic scar, sheltering a delightful hermitage, a relic from a forgotten age, leave the traveller stunned by their beauty and with the memory of an unforgettable sight.

A majestic grandeur and a serene beauty arise from the gorge cut by rivers through the mountain massifs. Right : two views of the gorge of Tarn; below the Verdon Gorge.

CORNWALL AND THE ENGLISH COAST

It comes as no surprise to learn that the largest island in Europe possesses an exceptional assortment of coasts. It is they indeed that represent the most beautiful landscapes, especially on the southern and western shores of England, here particularly sheer and indented.

The high cliffs of Dover resemble slices of a huge cretaceous cake, balancing those of Caux and Etretat in France. They are remarkable for their whiteness, which has earned the name of "Albion" (*alba* in Latin means "white") for this piece of land whose dazzling white coast was the first to be seen by navigators or by the invaders from Normandy.

Consisting of sheer cliffs, indented with what the Scottish would call "firths", and bordered with islands such as the Isle of Wight, the south coast of England aligns its rocky scars, emphasized by some famous names: Hastings, memorable for its famous battle; Brighton, home of the lofty Regency elegance of the 19th century; Portsmouth, the principal English naval base, where Dickens was born, and where Conan Doyle gave birth to Sherlock Holmes; Southampton, an important ocean port with a

medieval quarter which was miraculously spared during the bombardments of the last war. As for the rocky headland of Portland, sometimes rather grandly called the "Gibraltar of Wessex", it is certainly worthy of comparison with the famous rock.

The coast of Devon is so well protected from the westerly squalls that its climate seems almost like that of the riviera; and Torquay, set within an amphitheatre of seven hills, is the elegant centre of an unexpected and luxuriant British "côte d'azur". After the last large town in Devon, Plymouth, the Cornish coast begins, the most rugged, the wildest and the most extensive of all.

Cornwall is England's Brittany. A land of legends, of menhirs and of cromlechs; a Celtic world, confined, mysterious and secretive, Cornwall is a coastal area, looking out on all sides towards the high seas. For the tourists, it is the coast that they flock to. Amongst the numerous rocky projections that interrupt this tormented coastline, St. Michael's Mount, which draws to its picturesque setting both mystics and painters, is a perfect replica of Mont Saint-Michel on the French coast, also battered by the waves at high tide, and topped by a monastery dominating the mount.

But the highlight of a visit to Cornwall must be the headland of Tintagel, near Newquay, on the north coast of Cornwall, beside the Bristol Channel, the sheer drop of dark rock, sinister and menacing, which could well be used as the setting for a performance of a Wagner opera, or even of a Shakesparean tragedy. Indeed, the ruined castle that from the height of the cliff, eaten into by the constant buffeting of the waves, dominates the panorama of a formidable seascape, is the home of the famous King Arthur, who was in fact probably born here, according to certain historians of the 5th century. Which only goes to prove that in certain high places, blessed by the gods it is not even possible to disentagle legend from history! And one is tempted to dream, on the edge of this cliff, where the gentle Yseult so we are told, awaited, the return of Tristan.

England. Left : the rocks of Bedruthan Steps, in Cornwall. Above : the high cliffs of Dover which, because of their dazzling whiteness, earned England the name of "Albion". Right, a place steeped in legend : the castle of Tintagel on the sheer rocks of the headland of the same name.

the Irish Sea and supported by the spine of the Cambrian mountains. The coastline, the countryside, the hills, all is quiet and peaceful here. One is tempted to used the word "ecological", so rich is this Celtic land, where the Saxons drove back the last autochtons, in trout-streams burbling down the mountainside; Caernarvon and its illustrious Royal Castle; Barmouth, standing in a picturesquely dominant situation on the estuary of the Mawddach; the Snowdon massif 1,080 metres), the banks of the River Wye; Devil's Bridge and the turbulent waters of its canyon; the rock of Harlech Castle, constitute the essential features standing out on the Welsh landscape.

Further north, the area of Cumberland, which stretches out towards the Irish Sea along Morecambe Bay, is a vast eruptive relief, which has adopted the shape of a star, with nine valleys radiating out from the centre, each with one or several lakes; hence the name of the "Lake District" which has been given to the area. A long wall, built by the Emperor Hadrian in Roman times, runs across the country, stretching up and down the hills, whose melancholy mounds, veiled in mist, lend themselves to poetic tendencies. Wordsworth, Shelley and Coleridge especially loved these gentle landscapes, mournful and romantic, where the mirrors of the calm lakes, between Carlisle and Appleby, reflect the large, round humpedbacks of the Cambrian Mountains, over which the wind seems to whisper the poets' lines.

Wales : a view over the countryside, with the Menay Bridge, seen from Anglesey (left). A landscape in Cumberland (right). The estuary of the Mawddach, near Barmouth (below).

THE ENGLISH COUNTRYSIDE

While the coastline of England is often spectacular and can even in places be breathtakingly moving, the English countryside is most frequently nothing if not pleasant and restful. Yet certain counties have a strong personality of their own, making a visit to them an experience of pure delight.

Cornwall overwhelms the visitor by the impressive beauty of its coast, whereas Devon offers inland scenery which is absolutely delightful; the moorland of Dartmoor, the undulating high plateau, populated only by wild poneys and covered with short bristly grass, constantly ruffled by the never-failing wind. From Dartmouth to Exeter, the melancholy landscape of these moors crisscrossed with streams where copper and tin were worked for thousands of years, and where the Phoenicians came to get their supplies of mineral ore as far back as the eighth century B.C.

The infinite variety of the colours range through all the different shades of yellow and rust to highlight the infinite perspectives of this mournful landscape, deserted and bare, unexpected in a land so densely populated, and a spectacular sight. Appreciating perfectly the fantastic, supernatural and mysterious atmosphere of this chilly, captivating landscape, Conan Doyle situated the action of his famous novel "The Hound of the Baskervilles" there.

Another enclave, set in timeless wastes, other heather-covered moors, on the desolate mountains of the Pennine range, around Haworth, which inspired Emily Brontë to write "Wuthering Heights", devoted as she was to the rough romantic solitude emanating from the dramatic atmosphere of these northern wastes.

The Chedlar Gorge, in Somerset, a touristic highlight of the South-West, is perhaps the wildest spot in the whole of England. Sheer rock-faces, 200 metres high, worn away into caves or stiff with stalactites, with small stretches of grazing land for sheep on the top, producing a famous type of cheese, hem in a deeply cut passage, through which the road winds its way, in a setting which looks more like the American West than the peaceful English countryside.

Wales is a vast mountainous peninsula, washed by

THE SCOTTISH LOCHS, THE ISLE OF SKYE, THE GIANTS' CAUSEWAY

The Scottish Highlands in the county of Inverness, a world of minerals moulded by the waters and the glaciations of long ago, have broken up their granite, sparkling with mica, in the Atlantic, thus forming one of the most indented coastlines and as picturesque as any to be found anywhere. The waters of the ocean pound into enormous temperamental channels, pushing their way right into the midst of the higher land, covered with desolate moorland and bleak pastures. Thus were created the "lochs", corresponding to the Breton "abers" and the Norwegian "fjords".

It required several tens of millions of years to arrive at the present state of rocky chaos, carved out and moulded by earthquakes and landslides on different occasions. Certain of these lochs are better known than others: Loch Ness, for example, whose murky bluey-green waters are supposed to hide a phantom monster; the romantic Loch Assynt, in a stark landscape of grey gneiss, with layers of red sandstone; Loch Nevis and Loch Morar, set within banks which are particularly hilly and indented; or

through the green carpet of the high meadows. And it is this same type of geological formation, layers of tertiary volcanic basalt, that is the basis for the "Giants' Causeway" on the north coast of Ireland.

The rapid cooling of the flow of lava was the reason for their fragmentation into a mosaic of vertical prisms. Wind and sea erosion completed the work of cutting away, over thousands of years, to produce the breathtaking promontory as it stands today: a unique collection over a distance of 300 metres of basaltic prisms, most of them hexagonal, but some with four, five, eight or even ten faces, create a sight which is world-famous, and rightly so.

Scotland. Below and right, bottom : two different views of the Isle of Skye, one, taken in the month of May, with a rich spring growth relieving its ruggedness. Opposite : Loch Duich and the castle of Eilyan, in the county of Inverness. Below : a view of the "Giants' Causeway", huge blocks of stone, volcanic in origin.

Loch Hourn, whose nickname of "Hell's Lake" certainly aptly suggests the mysterious atmosphere, tinged with something of the supernatural, which hangs ominously over these lonely, secret waters.

Facing this eminently picturesque north-west coast of Scotland, and separated from it by a narrow channel only about 400 to 800 metres in width, stands the amazing Isle of Skye. If one can measure its length as stretching over a hundred kilometres, it is, on the other hand, impossible to give a definite measurement for the width, because of the infinite number of headlands and peninsulas all along the coastline. To such an extent that nowhere is one at more than eight kilometres from the sea, the element that formed it and remains the source of its livelihood.

A spine of grass-covered, wind-swept hills, none of them reaching a height of over 800 metres, runs down in disorderly fashion to offer the impressive sight of a rugged, jagged coast, plunging down into the ocean from the top of splendid brown cliffs. For if the hills inland have the noble texture of granite, with its twinkling specks of mica, the sea cliffs consist of a slice of dark basalt, wearing away into black pebbles, which form unusually funereal beaches along the coast. In May, however, the harshness and gloomy blackness of the shore, often shrouded in mist, is lit up by a sudden burst of spring colour, as thousands of little wild flowers push their way out

THE DUTCH CANALS,
WATTENZEE AND THE FRIESIAN ISLANDS
THE CLIFFS OF THE ISLE OF MØN

"God created the world, but the Dutch have created the Netherlands!" This saying contains an element of real truth: it was as a result of the permanent battle that is being fought by men to recuperate their land from the North Sea that the Dutch countryside has taken on its most original aspect. Except for the long, straight coastline, made up, from the Hague to Den Helder, of the most magnificent beach of white sand, backed by rolling dunes, which provide a natural dyke and protect the tulip-fields from the raging winds and waves of the sea, the rest of the "flat country" is worn away and eaten into by water. Huge rivers which meet there, and the onslaught of the sea as it rushes in. Under the protection of enormous dykes, a close network of canals has patiently been dug to drain the land, which has to be dried out unceasingly by a whole host of brightly-coloured windmills, using the force of the wind to make an ingenious system for pumping the water out work.

The region of Giethorn is the masterpiece of this stretch of nature with water predominating, the successful achievement of a delightful watery world created by man. Canals replace streets and reach each of the traditional light wooden houses, composing an idyllic country scene, charming and peaceful, where man appears to be at ease and very much part of the scenery, as much, indeed, as the herons that

one can observe as they lie in wait for frogs, green patches of colour as they leap in search of the shelter of clumps of rushes and water-lily leaves.

North of Holland, the ring of the Friesian Islands encircles a narrow strip of the North Sea, half imprisoned since the great dyke has closed the former Zuider Zee and has refused it access to the Ijsselmeer, which has gradually been transformed into polders. Thus was created the "Wattenzee", a strange and secret inland sea, so shallow that at each low tide the Baltic as it withdraws uncovers an unusual world of marshy shoals, crisscrossed with the haphazard patterns of odd little channels. An unreal universe, sparkling in the rays of the setting sun, and the exclusive realm of birds, digging in the mud with their beaks, in search of their supper. There is talk of joining the island of Friesland by means of dykes, and drying out the Wattenzee to transform it in its turn into one of those chequerboard patterns of geometrically arranged plantations, which are not lacking either in grandeur nor in a kind of poetry in spite of their artificiality. Meanwhile, the islands remain some of the most remote and unspoilt in Europe. Ameland, Vlieland and especially Terschelling, always impress their rare visitors with their harsh and rugged beauty, untouched and like something out of another world.

Texel is the best known. Called also "Eierland", the island of eggs, it is a paradise for birds and an ornithological reserve which has no equal; gulls of all kinds, spoonbills, swans, wild geese, and even occasional flamingoes, have made their homes here in this

spot, an oasis for them in the midst of the buffeting of the sea and wind.

In May and June, at brooding time, all the beautiful world of our feathered, cheeping friends, the large migratory birds, monopolize the marshy hollows set among the dunes, the domain of the sheep that still occupy the hundred or so old sheepfolds scattered about all over the island.

Very different is the sight of the chalky cliffs of the Isle of Mon, to the south-east of the Danish archipelago. Planed down by the glaciations, their very pure secondary cretaceous layers fall into the Baltic in the form of immaculately white cliffs, about a hundred metres high, startlingly bright and bordered with a slender glacis of silex.

Above : the cliffs of Mons Klint, to the east of the charming island of Mon, in Denmark, and a characteristic landscape in Holland. Opposite : dunes on the shore of the North Sea.

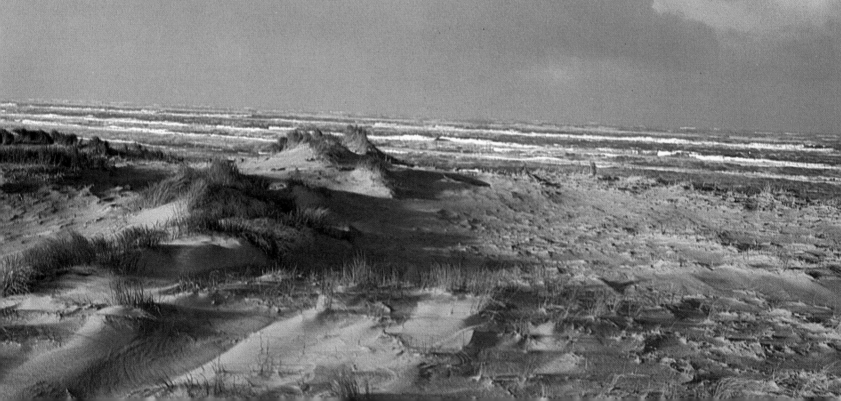

THE VALLEY OF THE RHINE
KÖNIGSSEE, THE DACHSTEIN MASSIF
AND LAKE HALSTATT

The Rhine, the longest river in Europe (1,300 kilometres long) and the most powerful (2,200 m³ at its estuary), has an amazing destiny. Rising, like the Rhone, in the St. Gothard massif, at an altitude of 2,000 metres, it rushes down to 270 metres at Basel. That means that at the beginning of its course it is a real Alpine torrent ! Then, further along its way, leaving behind its early bed which led it towards the west and the Saone, it suddenly changes direction. Turning directly north, between the Jura and the Black Forest, it starts upon the middle part of its journey, making a difficult passage for itself through the Taunus hills, before become a large winding river flowing across the plains. Separating into several different arms, it finally loses all its personality by mingling with the waters of the Meuse in a vast delta around Rotterdam.

In the middle of its course, it is a royal legendary river, not only serving as a frontier between countries but also having a historical destiny, with the economic and cultural importance of a great connecting link between Germanic Europe and the North Sea.

During its crossing of the Taunus, beyond the confluent with the Neckar then the Main, it cuts into the schist by means of a « heroic breach », a place of pilgrimage for the Romantics and the cradle of Germanic legends. The famous rocky pinnacle of the Loreleï, the spectacular and mythological setting for a legend sung by Heine, symbolises the vocation of the Rhine as a sacred river of Germanic culture. Narrow here (300 metres) and very deep, it bathes with its dark mysterious waters a number of delightful wooded islands, between the shores on which well-kept elegant vines rise up in tiers, under the watchful eye of the old hieratic feudal "burgs", crumbling yet still proudly erect.

"Burgs", feudal, hieratic sentinels, rooted to the spot and intractable, their medieval stones seem to be protecting "The Rhine Gold" and sheltering the phantom shades of the vaporous Walkyries.

The miracle is that it has been able to reconcile this commercial and political role with a poetic vocation which has fortunately been preserved and handed on over the centuries.

In the heart of the Bavarian Alps, an Austrian enclave which only became part of Germany in 1809, Königssee, as its name indicates ("the king's lake") is the most beautiful watery landscape in the Bavarian mountains. The striking beauty of the setting results from the contrast between a luminous stretch of glacial water, stretching over a distance of 8 kilometres the unexpected, winding bends of an Alpine fjord, and the brightness of the high light-coloured chalky cliffs in which it is set. There are boat trips on the lake, to discover breathtaking views of the high mountain scenery, which acts as a

Left : the curious church of St. Bartholomew, on the banks of the Königsee; right : the shore of this lake. Below : Austria : the famous Halstatt on the banks of the lake of the same name, and the massif of the Dachstein, standing aloft over the Gosausee.

remarkable snowcovered backcloth. Thus one passes close to the foot of the Kehlstein spur, at the summit of which Hitler installed his famous "eagle's nest", accessible by a vertiginous road, winding its way up round hairpin bends, from which one can discover the quintessence of the Bavarian Alps.

On the borders of the provinces of Salzburg and Styria, the Dachstein is a high glacial plateau, a sort of Alpine high altitude "causse", desolate and deserted. It is dominated by the imposing massif of the same name, a huge grey limestone base imprisoning between its sheer rock-faces an impressive glacier with extraordinary seracs, the largest and the most beautiful in the Austrian Alps.

This magnificent immaculately pure mountain has several icy grottos hollowed out in it, grottos which are amongst the most magically enchanting in the world:the "Mammoth Grotto", with its kilometres of caves lined with walls of ice and the "Ice Giant's Grotto", decorated with columns and frozen water-falls.

On the north face of the massif, the name of Halstatt, already known to prehistorians as the cradle of an original proto-historic culture, would also deserve to be known for the grandiose beauty of its lake, a pure and limpid mirror of blue water, in which is reflected the unreal image of this universe of crystal.

Germany. On these pages, several different views of the valley of the Rhine. Below : the castles of Stolzenfels, Sterrenberg and Liebenstein. Right : Gutenfels Castle dominates the river and the "Pfalz", standing in the middle of the river, at Kaub.

THE MATTERHORN, THE JUNGFRAU, AND THE EIGER

However blasé one may be, the sight of the Matterhorn (or Cervin) in the centre of the Pennine Alps is unique and exciting.

Standing on the frontier between three countries (France, Italy and Switzerland), between three cultures and three languages, it raises high above the Alpine pastures its impressive sharp rocky peak, also marking the line of demarcation between the valley of the Po and the valley of the Rhone. It is not, however, entirely to its geographical characteristics that it owes its universal fame and renown. If it has become the symbol of the Mountain, with a capital M, for all those who love mountains and mountaineering, this widespread reputation is due to the ideal combination of several different elements: the fascinating aesthetical beauty of this rocky pyramid, with its icy flanks and its slender peaks, as sharp as the cutting edge of a blade.

Its isolation also adds to its majesty, making it seem to rise higher, in regal fashion, far from all other mountains which might otherwise compete with it, and to rule alone and uncontested over a peaceful world of pastoral valleys, in which are clustered the delightfull villages of Valtournanche and the Breuil.

Lastly, let us mention its history, filled with passionate and tragic events, inextricable from the history of alpinism from its origins when, during the 19th century, the Alpine range was seething with fabulous exploits of great courage. In such conditions, it was inevitable that the young Edward Whymper, having discovered and been overwhelmed by the fascination of this unique, magnificent mountain, unlike any other in the world, should at the age of twenty, in 1860, decide that he must climb it, becoming so obsessed with the idea that he could think of nothing else. He did in fact climb it, reaching the summit on 14th August, after a memorable ascension, performed in a state of triumphant euphoria, before ending in a dramatic manner, when the party slipped, breaking the cord that dragged four members of the expedition down to their deaths.

The famous trio of the Jungfrau, The Monch and the Eiger, form the backbone of the Bernese Alps. The Jungfrau, meaning "young woman" or "virgin", because of the immaculate purity of its snows, and because of its resistance to man's approach, is indeed difficult to climb, though the summit was first successfully reached by the Meyer brothers in 1811. It is a massive pyramid, reaching an altitude of 4,166 metres, huge and weighty compared with the Matterhorn. It owes its attraction and fame to an amazing little cog-railway, built between 1896 and 1912, which runs right up to the highest station in Europe, the "Jungfraujoch", at 3,454 metres, 700 metres below the summit, thus allowing "tourists" to venture into the forbidden world of the high peaks.

The Eiger for its part offers a completely different aspect, that of the very high mountains reserved for specialists. Its north face, although not very high (3,975 metres), relatively speaking, is a combination of all the technical difficulties on a very high level. Its overhanging rocks, worn away by the constant washing of the rain, and cut by hanging stretches of ice, is a terrifying wall, enclosing all the possible dangers of mountaineering.

Above : view on the Mönch and the Jungfrau. Right : the Cervin. A stark, bare look; a cold, pure beauty.

MAZURY, THE CARPATHIANS, LAKE BALATON AND THE DANUBE

Behind the shores of the Baltic, lined with dunes and a paradise for sea-birds, the land that is now part of Poland, formed by the Scandinavian glaciers of prehistoric times, offers some pleasant countryside, with gently-rolling hills, covered with magnificent forests, and dotted with a multitude of little lakes. Mazury, a continuation of Pomerania, on the border of the U.S.S.R., consists of striking landscapes, very similar to neighbouring Finland, but much less familiar and more barren and sparsely populated. In spite of the difficult task of trying to till such unfertile soil and the fact that it was almost impossible to make a way into the forests, this was the site of the first Slav settlement, on both sides of the river Vistula, in the hinterland of Gdansk (Dantzig). The romantic course of the river Radunia and the "land of a thousand lakes" in Mazury are a delight to the eye. In fact, there are more than two thousand lakes covering an area of more than 10,000 square metres, which sparkle in the pale sunshine as it permeates the countryside and its lakes with that special delicate and fleeting Scandinavian light, showing the pastel shades off to their best advantage.

To the south of Poland, and on the border with Czechoslovakia, the mighty mountain range of the Carpathians is split by the Dunajec gorge. Over a distance of nine kilometres, the river, which runs down to join the Vistula downstream from Cracow, beats up against the lofty Jurassic limestone cliffs that imprison it. In the narrowest places, the rugged channel is no more than 300 metres across. It is a micro region that has been authentically preserved.

The soul of Hungary is the plain with horizons stretching to infinity. In this fascinating steppe of the Putza region, picturesque Magyar cow-herds still lead their herds to drink at anachronistic hand pumps, recalling the empty yet constantly stirring wide open spaces of nearby Central Asia.

The main tourist centre remains Lake Balaton, extending over a length of 78 kilometres and a width of from 5 to 15 kilometres, its 600 square kilometres making it one of the largest lakes in Europe. Sometimes a precious opalescent or emerald-green mirror, fringed with reeds, sometimes foaming with tumultuous dark waves, roused by the wind from the steppes, and sometimes a polar world frozen by the icy winter blasts, it is always a sight to be enjoyed, ever-changing and spellbinding in its poetic intensity and its nostalgic languour.

The Danube is a river of infinite variety. Along its 2,800 kilometres of winding course, how many different landscapes and how many different climates it passes through, between the Black Forest of its source and its mouth opening into the sea opposite the Crimea! Freed from the restraint of the Balkans and the Transylvanian Alps, at the remarkable narrow straits of the "Gates of Iron", it lets itself flow on towards the Black Sea, seemingly without any other purpose but to act as the frontier between Bulgaria and Roumania. Beyond Galati, it divides into three separate arms, going off in very different directions, so that they are as much as a hundred kilometres apart at their estuaries, forming a huge delta, unlike any other in the world in size and in the atmosphere that it produces.

Left, top : on the banks of Lake Balaton, an important touristic spot in Hungary, Mount Badacsony. Below : pastureland in the Tatras mountains, in Poland. Opposite : the Dunaja Gorge (Poland).

IN THE HEART OF THE IMMENSITY
OF RUSSIA

The immensity of the territory of the U.S.S.R. is a real-house of exceptional natural phenomena, which are, alas, difficult and wearisome to reach, because of the enormous distances that have to be covered and the uncertainty of the means of transport. For it is to the very heart of the mountainous massifs or desert-like stretches of country that one must go to find these remarkable landscapes.

The desert of Kara Koum is one of the most impressive in the world. Occupying the south-west corner of the country, it corresponds to the former depression where the gigantic prehistorical Caspian used to spread, now the territory of Turkestan. As is the case with the Sahara, the towns are laid out on the edge of the desert, as if they were harbours. But caravans no longer cross this immense desolate area, covering more than 600,000 km²; a land of sand, where a constantly-blowing wind never ceases to harass the dunes, and hollow out ridges that are for ever being rearranged, at the mercy of the blustery gusts. Yet, after the scanty spring rainfall, the desert flowers and produces a surprising, but ephemeral, green carpet.

Near the edge of the Caspian, the range of the great Balkhans, dotted with a multitude of geysers and warm springs, with deposits of crusty salt and strange eroded shapes, has an attractive kind of austere grandeur.

The intensely blue mirror of the sea of Aral, set within these surroundings, is so vast (66,000 km²) that it is subject to tides and familiar with fierce storms. It represents the remains of the Caspian after the glaciations and owes its survival simply to the two great rivers that flow into it, the Syr-Daria and the Amou Daria, whose enormous deltas bring down such a quantity of alluvial mud that the banks advance several metres each year. Sparsely inhabited, for there are few fish, it is a half-dead sea, yet full of charm and with an air of melancholy.

Lake Baikal presents a completely different aspect. It is set in a deep fault scarring the heart of Central Asia, on the borders of Mongolia, with an S-shaped mark, 640 kilometres long by 80 kilometres wide. Its depth (1,500 metres) makes it the largest reservoir of fresh water in the world, (23,000 km³) and an outstanding fishing reserve. It is difficult to imagine such a mass of liquid, as vast as the whole of Belgium, hemmed in by 2,000-metre-high mountains, covered with a "Taiga" planted with conifer trees: this results in a micro-climate where the extremes of temperature are very close together (−15 to +13) compared with those of nearby Siberia where the temperature ranges from −30 to +20.

The Caucasus, whose very name evokes an atmosphere of legend, is a formidable range of Alpine type, between the Black Sea and the Caspian, stretching from the Crimean peninsula to the Iranian plateau. An intermingling of different massifs, including the Elbrouz, which is the best-known, the Caucasus is

not only a geographical barrier, difficult to cross, but also a cultural refuge for the ethnic groups who take shelter within its folds.

The Darial Gorge is the key to Georgia and the real gateway to the Caucasus.

The course of the river Terek has hollowed out there a most impressive rift, down which it flows with great difficulty along its tortured bed, on its way towards the sea, held in on either side by two steep faces, rising sheer up to a height of 1,400 metres. This

U.R.S.S. Top, left : in the Caucasus, Lake Ritsa. Above : a view of the vast stretch of water of Lake Baïkal in the heart of Central Asia. Left : the Don.

THE FINNISH LAKES AND
THE LOFOTEN ISLANDS

Finland has lakes scattered all over its territory. They are the result of the erosion that was produced over a period of millions of years by the Scandinavian glacial shield. This myriad of lakes, both large and small, lying in confusion all over the country, can really only be appreciated to the full from the air. This is an area that, because of its flatness, only allows rare general views, so that the very slightest of hills, even measuring only 20 metres, seems to be an outstanding belvedere, revealing lake-studded landscapes that are amongst the finest in the world: with superb forests, remarkable for the striking straightness of the rows of trees, with their reddish or silvery tints. And the sparkling mirrors of the water, so limpid and reflecting so perfectly the pines and birches that one cannot help wondering which is the reflection and which is the real picture. With such a vast number of lakes, it is difficult to choose the most beautiful. Perhaps the finest are to be found spread out along the Russian frontier, and in the middle of southern Finland. The 1,400 km² of Lake Saimao, seven times as large as that of Lake Geneva, were linked in 1850 to the Baltic by means of a canal constructed with 28 locks over a distance of 56 kilometres. Its banks are magnificently indented and wooded islands rise in disorder here and there, looking like little green cushions floating on the waters. The Lakes Paipinne, Kivijarvi, Peilinen and Inati, are so many masterpieces achieved by nature.

But the pearl of all this region is, without any doubt, the natural dyke of Pankaharju, the crest of an ancient moraine, running across Lake Puruvesi. The journey along it offers the finest views in Finland. From this incomparable belvedere, one can discover what is perhaps one of the most beautiful landscapes in the world. The different seasons and hours of the day take upon themselves the responsibility for making them an even more breathtaking sight; the flaming autumn tints, colouring the paleness of the beech-trees with a startlingly bright auburn wig; the sunsets, setting the forest on fire with their magical glowing colours; the endless winter, dusting the dark fir-woods with frosty spangles and little puffs of snow; and most striking of all, the endless light days of summer, lighting the fires of the midnight sun, a huge Japanese lantern swinging on the misty horizon, stirring up superb braziers of burning embers.

At 68" latitude north, beyond the polar circle, the Lofoten islands are the most accessible and amongst the most beautiful of all the Arctic islands. The archipelago, steep highlands, formed by the quaternary erection of the Scandinavian Alps, is a confused cluster of little island amongst the many fjords

It is in Finland that one finds the most famous lake landscapes in the world. Above : Lake Saïmaa and its little wooded islands. Left : another lake, at Outo Kumpu.

carved in a labyrinth of capes and headlands. The approach by sea is really spectacular and one can admire from afar, long before reaching it, the formidable wall, a crenelated mineral fortress of sharp, jagged peaks. They appear on the horizon, sometimes wrapped in cotton-wool clouds, sometimes hardly distinguishable through the long veils of mist, and sometimes lost in the downpour of a heavy shower, brightened here and there with the dazzling shades of a rainbow.

Two different views of the Lofoten Islands, a rugged, barren sight with their rocks which can produce so little vegetation. In places these rocky cliffs can reach a height of as much as 1 000 metres.

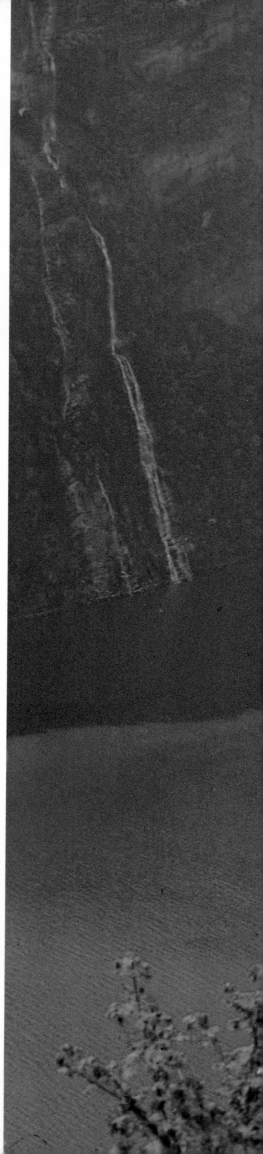

THE FJORDS, AND THE WATERFALLS OF NORWAY

For millions of years Scandinavia remained covered with a carapace of glaciers, firmly implanted in the granite base forming the substratum of this "inlandsis".

The end of glaciation and the melting of the glaciers brought to light moraines, which were soon invaded by the sea, giving rise to "fjords", deep very indented gulfs, worn away by erosion. The most famous and the most spectacular of these glacial valleys are to be found in Norway, where they scallop the coasts from Stavanger to Kirkenes.
The best known and the most outstanding, stopping-points not to be missed on all organized trips, are grouped along the west-central coast, between Bergen and Bödö, below the Arctic Circle. They eat into the mountain base which makes up the backbone of the country, making incredible inroads into it, seeming to stretch into infinity, sometimes reaching a length of more than a hundred kilometres.

Others are equally famous: the huge Nordfjord, a vast expanse of sea, which acts as a natural theatre for the fiery wonder of the Scandinavian sunset; the Sögnefjord, the longest in Norway, displaying its rocky lacework over a distance of 180 kilometres; the modest, unspoilt Söfjord and Eidfjord, havens of peaceful undisturbed beauty, producing the magical and alchemical synthesis of rock, light and water.

Yet it is perhaps above the Arctic Circle that the fjords offer their most fascinating and exhalting spectacle, magnified by the incomparable illumination of summers that have no night. Who knows the Lyngenfjord where a formidable barrier of high peaks, perpetually covered with ice and neve? The Gleenfjord or the Oxfjord? Wild and sublime inlets in the Finnmark coast, in Lapp territory, visited each evening by the flaming red midnight sun, infinitely more beautiful in this geological setting, which has remained unchanged since the beginning of creation, than on the sad uninteresting promontory of the North Cape, swarming with thousands of invading tourists.

It is impossible to dissociate the fjords from their surrounding glaciers and waterfalls. The former represent the beautiful remains of the primitive glacial shield, since the Hardanger, and more important still, the Jostedai, are the most extensive in Europe. As for the waterfalls, there are such an infinite number of them that any fjord-side road will surprise you with magnificent, anonymous delights.

Norway. Above : The coast near the port of Narvik, which is free of ice all the year. Below : a view of the Vöringfoss. Right : in the fjord of Geiranger, the fairylike synthesis of rock, light and water.

shores of immense Greenland, the largest island in the world, veritable Arctic continent, one comes here to enjoy the ice, the inspired architect of extraordinary structures, stunning in their absolute purity and ethereal whiteness.

Greenland; the fjord of ice at Jakobshavn (left) and, below, in the midnight sun. Left, bottom: the hard face of a glacier of Spitzberg. Right: Iceland, an eruption of the volcano Heimaey and one of the very numerous geysers in the country, signs of a vulcanism that is still active.

ICELAND, SPITZBERG, GREENLAND

Iceland—a real land of ice— floats like a mirage on the mists of the northern Atlantic, mysterious and strange. Like an open-air geological museum, it exhibits to the ever-increasing number of visitors a series of Dantesque landscapes, fantastic basins where the elements—earth, water and fire—combine to make up a haunting, spectacular island.

It is difficult to reach, lost in the harshness of the meteorological conditions of the great north, and seems only to have been colonized about 874 by Viking explorers from Norway. The traveller who approaches it by passing first through its capital, Reykjavik (meaning "the bay of vapours") is not reassured for long by the restful sight of wooden dwellings in Scandinavian style, painted in startlingly bright colours to cheer up the greyness of the interminable northern twilights. All around, nature is seething and stirring. For it is rather "Fireland" than "Iceland" that the island should be called. Almost two hundred volcanos have expanded this outpost of hell, shaken each year by several hundred earthquakes (which means almost one a day!). A tenth of the country is covered with lava flows and fields of solidified lava. The largest of them stretches over an area of 4,000 square kilometres, at the foot of the most important crater, the Vatnajökull, the

starting-point of an exceptional volcanic range, which broke out in eruption in 1783, in a cloud of ashes which buried houses and pastureland under more than 10 km³ of lava.

Iceland, a real museum of vulcanology, can offer every type of crater possible. Among the most famous are the Snaefellsjökull, through which Jules Verne had his heroes pass on their way towards the centre of the earth: the Askja, filled with a turquoise lake in the very heart of a desolate region, so much like some landscape on the moon that it has been used as a training ground for American cosmonauts. The Elekla, whose long ridge of a hundred eruptions has taken on the appearance of a mountain of fire, terrifying the ancient navigators who believed it to be the gates of hell, even taking the rumblings of the crater for the groaning of the condemned. This volcanic activity is everywhere, in the form of smoke-holes, boiling hot springs and bubbling waters. The geysers represent the most spectacular display of the universal vulcanism of the island.

There are also, in contrast, glaciers in Iceland, but the most marvellous are undoubtedly in Spitzberg and in Greenland, in spite of its name.

Whether it be to the west coast, the Svalbard archipelago, situated at a distance of 600 kilometres beyond the North Cape, which was once the home of Dutch and Norwegian whale-catchers. or the western

CAPE ST. VINCENT AND SAGRES

A massive mountainous promontory, hemming in the south side of the basin of the Tagus and ending right in the ocean with Cape Espichel, the Serra da Arrabida is a setting of high reliefs, harsh, wild and rugged. It runs down into a sea as blue as the Mediterranean, with its red jagged cliffs, towering to a height of 500 metres, and its peak covered with a sparse vegetation, stunted and spindly, continually buffeted by the wind coming off the sea. The superb coastal road high up overlooking the sea, following its crest, offers impressive aerial views of the indented coastline, an elegant rocky lacework fringed with foam, in which nestle delightful little creeks.

The highlight of Portuguese tourism is, however, its superb south coast. It starts on the Atlantic-facing side with the remarkable Cape St. Vincent. Its solid rocky form, stretching out towards the open sea, where nothing interrupts the view right out to the horizon of sea joining sky, cuts like the prow of a ship through the rolling blue waves which once witnessed the departure of the caravelles of the great explorers. The impact and the majesty of the setting had already made their impression on the people of ancient times, who set it aside as a sacred spot where the gods came to rest, watching the sun set in the sea, beyond the last known lands. The Cape, the point farthest west in Europe, represented also the end of the world until the 15th century, the "sacred promontory", the advance post and watchtower of ancient western civilization. It is now occupied by an old fort, and still seems to be waiting and watching for possible invaders, consisting of a remarkable seascape, which never fails to produce an impression of intensity and grandeur. The cold solid strenght of the bare rock, the ocean stretching into infinity, the surface of the water ruffled by the Gulf Stream currents, touching the European continent here for the first time, the constantly changing sky, often stormy then quickly bright again, and the blasts of wind meting out their punishment without mercy on the vegetation which stubbornly tries to resist its onslaught, all this gives an atmosphere of elation and mystical transcendence. One can thus understand quite well that the body of St. Vincent, martyrized by Diocletian, was hidden here in a hollow in the reef which extends the Cape, under the protection of the waves and the sea-birds.

A short distance from there, but on the Mediterranean side of the peninsula, the headland of Sagres reaches out its flat, wind-swept cape, prettily described as "a huge paw lying on the velvet of the sea". Another "land's end", barren and stripped of all vegetation, this dominant acropolis of extremely jagged reddish cliffs, stands on the edge of a sheer drop into the spray of the splashing foam below. It is the home of seagulls and crows, which keep alive the memory of the infante Henri "the navigator", the inspired forerunner of the great discoveries. He retired to this promontory at the beginning of the 14th century and died there in 1460, after ten years spent inventing the basic requirements for modern navigation, in the midst of the best cartographers and sailors of his time.

On the Atlantic coast of Portugal, the prestigious Cape St. Vincent (above). This is the farthest point west in Europe. Left : a view of the beautiful countryside of the Alentejo. Right : the Portuguese coast, near Setubal.

THE MARISMAS DEL GUADALQUIVIR AND LANZAROTE

Formerly a vast gulf, the mouth of the Guadalquivir, gradually cut off from the sea by a barrier of dunes, has now become an immense stretch of marshy land. A haphazard network of canals with strangely meandering bends separates a mosaic of sedimentary islands, alluvial, immobile rafts, of boggy consistency, seeming to float on the surface of the stagnant waters, within the sensuous arms of the river. These "marismas" (marshes), make up a strange but attractive aquatic universe, remote and out of this world, as if time has stood still, unmoved by the agitation and excitement of the Andalusia that surrounds it. This humid, peaceful group of lagoons encloses an area reserved for lonely pasture-land on which can be found the last herds of wild horses and the most famous breeding-centres for the brave "toros", intended for the ritual of bull-fighting. It is difficult to imagine that there used to be some-where on these shores the fabulous Tartessos. A legendary mythical, city, Eldorado, in the west, which was the wealthy colony and trading-post of the Phoenicians, the masters and merchants of the ancient Mediterranean, who came here to collect and commercialize the wealth to be found here. The "marismas" today are a protected ecological sanc-tuary, a sort of Andulasian Camargue. Submerged during the high water of winter, bursting into colour with the blossoming of flowers at each spring festival, breaking out into yellowish cracks under the baking hot summer sun, they remain a haven that has providentially been spared by man. In this natural temple, animals reign, along with the colonies of birds, who find the micro-climate an ideal stopping-place on their long flight as they migrate between Europe, of which these marginal regions are almost no longer a part, and Africa, of which they give promise.

Just like Portuguese Madeira, famous for its terraces and its luxuriant vegetation dominating the sea, the Spanish archipelago of the Canary Islands is a volcanic creation, set out in the Atlantic off the coast of Africa. It is the island of Lanzarote, more still than Tenerife, and even than the picturesque Gomera, that is the strangest and most unusual highlight of these "Islands of the Blest". Lying a thousand kilometres from the Spanish peninsula, this little island, constantly changing as a result of eruptions, is nothing but a heap of lava vomited by the powerful volcanic massif of the "mountain of fire", which make up the ossature and the main attraction of the island. The lava flow and the fields of lava which cover its slopes give the landscape a characteristic appearance. The beaches, here parti-cularly stark and hostile, and the narrow terraces perched on the volcano, all used to be covered with "*picons*", that infernal rain of lapilli, which fell from the sky in times past, and was spat out by the crater which has since calmed down its activity, though it is still impressive.

Left, top : the mouth of the Guadalquivir, in Spain. Left and right, three different views of the Canary Islands : Tenerife (the largest of the islands), Gomera and, from Lanzarote, a view over the island of Graciosa.

SIGHTS TO BE SEEN IN ANDALUSIA

There are some names that can make us dream, and Andalusia is one of them. A matchless region, heavy with the perfume of jasmine and the clicking of castanets, it is synonymous with Spain, corridas, *feria,* and flamenco. It continues to be endowed with an incredible power of evocation, and is steeped in myths of which Bizet's "Carmen", constantly being brought up to date, is the symbol and synthesis.

The Andalusian coast, forgetting that it was once a haven for navigators of ancient times —Greeks, Phoenicians or Carthaginians, as they sailed the Mediterranean, on which their lives depended—, has now been transformed into an uninterrupted seaside resort from Alicante to Gibraltar. The interior folds of the Sierras and the warm plain of the majestic Guadalquivir have conserved fabulous sites, the scene of the Moorish adventure which brought enlightenment to Spain and changed the whole of the western world.

It was in 711 that the Arabs from North Africa landed at Tarifa and founded a Moslem colony in Spain, a collection of emirates dependent on the Ommeyades of Damas. They remained there right up until 1492, centuries during which their influence spread, furthered by raids which took them to almost the whole of the peninsula, and even as far as Poitiers.

Andalusia built itself upon this zone of permanent occupation by the caliphs, a real Arab state, colonial and expanding.

Three towns were the jewels in the setting of the coast. They have preserved all that was magnificent in what Moslem art had produced, and present-day visitors still succomb to ther charm and fascination.

Cordova became the first independant caliphate in 929, under the control of Abd el Rahman. Its mosque is famous throughout the world and is striking in the gracefulness of its forest of columns and the preciosity of the finely-decorated doors, set into its ochre-coloured mass, in front of which stratches a pleasant patio.

Seville, its buildings clustered together on the banks of the legendary Guadalquivir, became the capital of the Almohad kingdom of Yacoub el Mansour. Its prosperity and its spreading influence led it to cover its territory with gardens and palaces. All that is left of the palace of the Almohads is a patio with slender arcades, but Peter the Cruel was also fascinated by this kind of art and, far from destroying the palace, even built another one, faithfully copied from the Arab model, thus inaugurating what was soon to become Mudejar art.

Even when building the striking cathedral, which was to commemorate the reconquest, the Christian architects could not free themselves from the subtle Moorish influence, and they respected the "Giralda", an old minaret, 98 metres high, delicately decorated, and characteristic of the style of the Almohads of Morocco, both refined and monumental.

Grenada, the last stronghold of the Arab presence in Spain, was only reconquered in 1492. Boabdil, its last master, according to a pleasant little legend, sighed with longing as he returned to take one last look at this dear Alhambra hill, where the pavilions in red stone emerged from a clump of cypresses. It must be admitted that this blessed hill, its summit girt by a strong defensive enclosure, is a perfect example of the aesthetic, almost sensual refinement of the Arab building. Each pavilion opens out on to an interior patio lined by a colonnade, elegant in its slenderness. Water, everywhere present, ripples and burbles in a kaleidoscope of fountains and opal and emeraldgreen pools.

The most impressive of these patios is the famous "Lions' Court", universally known, and with the rare particularity of being decorated with an animal design, which was forbidden by the Koran.

But everywhere, on the plains or in the Andalusian Sierras, other lesser-known towns, offer exceptio-

Andalusia. One of the "white villages", Algatocin, near Ronda (above), the tormented relief of the interior and the Sierra Nevada, enclosing the famous Alhambra of Grenada.

nal sights and monuments. Baeza and Ubeda, attractive art centres, abounding in Renaissance buildings, in baroque or plateresque style, in a sea of olive-trees spreading up the hills to the frontier of Don Quixote's La Mancha; Jerez de la Frontera, the home of sherry and the breeders of the brave fighting bulls; Antequera, a striking example of the white villages, dazzling in the sunshine; and lastly, Ronda, a dignified old town, perched high in the heart of the Sierra, situated astride a spectacular ravine separating the "Ciudad" into two sections. This is the cradle of the tauromarchy, and its arenas are the oldest in Spain.

It often happens in Spain that the perfect symbiosis between the architecture of the buildings and the surrounding countryside is an essential element of the beauty, the power to move and the majesty of the sites.

This es even more true of Andalusia than elsewhere, and its sumptuous Moorish mirages fit perfectly into a universe bathed in sunshine, where the olive-trees rustled by cicadas enclose white limewashed villages.

Spanish land, which was for centuries African land, here has kept all the musty odours of exoticism which are so attractive.

Andalusia. Top, left and bottom, right : two rural views of this amazing country. The two other photos on these pages show us new aspects of the "white village" (Ardales and, above, Gaucin).

THE ITALIAN LAKES AND
THE DOLOMITES

Stendhal pitied those who were not excited by the dreamlike landscapes offered by the tormented basins of the great lakes, cutting deeply into the Italian side of the Alps.

On the borders of Switzerland, a dramatic extension of the Lombardy plains, they provide a universal tourist attraction. The mildness of the microclimate guarantees them an abundance of luxuriant vegetation, both trees and flowers, making a sumptuous decoration contrasting strongly with the severity and harshness of the mountainous setting. Poets, painters, and artists from all over the world extol the beauties of this delightful region, so ideal for inspiring and fanning the ardour of the Romantic passions of the last century.

Lake Maggiore stretches over a distance of 65 kilometres its deep-blue mirror, though in winter the bad weather may sometimes stir up real tempests on the lake. From its waters rise the delightful Borromean islands, like four bright petals of a rich aquatic plant.

Lake Como, in the shape of a badly-written letter Y, stretches its three arms over 46 kilometres, into the hollows of the picturesque valleys of Lecco and Colico, between the high snow-covered peaks. Its banks are lined with a profusion of olive-trees, fruit-trees and exotic flowers, amongst which can be seen magnificent Renaissance villas and delightful baroque mansions, of which the flowered pergolas and the stone balustrades run right down to the edge of the water. The most famous amongst them are the Villa d'Este, built in 1598 for the ruling house which reigned over Ferrara and Modena, before being used as a lovenest for Caroline of Brunswick, the abandoned wife of King George IV; the Villa Carlotta, the elegant, luxurious residence of their daughter, Charlotte Augusta, married to Leopold of Saxony.

Lake Garda flirts with Venezia. It feels very deeply the influence of its eastern situation; set amongst vines, olive-trees, lemon-trees and agaves, it bathes in a pleasantly languorous torpor, in which picturesque fishing villages lie sleepily at the end of fjords of a very Mediterranean type, the whole setting looking like the scenery for an operetta.

To the east of the lake region, the Alps of the Upper Adige are transformed and completely change their character. More rugged massifs, rising to over 4,000 metres, more glaciers; bold reliefs, odd and unexpected, rise above pastoral valleys, like a blade being drawn from its sheath. The reason for this unique landscape is the fact that it consists of a soft chalky rock, called "dolomite", after the name of a French geologist, Dolomieu, who studied it closely. What is most striking about this region is the contrast between the welcoming charm of the valleys and the inhospitable, almost hostile, aspect of the slopes of the pink rocks, twisted into strange shapes by the fierce erosion of water and wind. The spectacular road through the Dolomites is perhaps the most beautiful in the Alps, revealing the most extraordinary landscapes; jagged mountain ridges, straight rock faces like the walls of a colossal citadel, giddy heights like a split blade, towering peaks which recall the Ahaggar.

Northern Italy : the charm of its lakes and its superb mountains. Above : the second of the Borromean Islands, set like jewels in Lake Maggiore. Below : a view of the Dolomites, at the foot of the Geissler Needles. Right : the Massif of the Sella.

THE HILLS OF TUSCANY

In the heart of Italy, Tuscany is a vast region, stretching out at the foot of the Apennines, right to the Mediterranean coast. This well-favoured area, covering a surface of 23,000 square kilometres, occupies a unique place in the heart of the lovers of beauty who visit the peninsula, so beloved by heroes and gods. Tuscany, land of history and art, enjoys an unequalled prestige throughout the world. It must be said that here nature has had to ally itself with all kinds of divinities to offer perfection and the quintessence of all that is beautiful. God and the earth seem to have united their efforts to provide the magnificent setting which serves as a display-case for the three hundred Tuscan towns and villages, each of them containing a store of fabulous treasures.

How can one, indeed, make a distinction here between Nature, Man's art and his History, so intimately linked in the fold of the earth kneaded and moulded like pottery? In Tuscany, the country itself is a pure masterpiece.

The raw materials for this wonderful countryside of Tuscany are nothing else but its hills. Not very high, rather ordinary in appearance, but drawn with smooth, languorous lines. As harmonious in their outlines as they are well-balanced in volume, they are already perfect in their proportions and their grace, like the domes and cupolas that they conceal in their folds. Planted with straggly olive-trees, or vines with their shoots bending elegantly like the arms of Oriental dancing girls, the hills integrate into their tawny soil the delicate lines of man's works. They even annex his habitat and are delighted to assimilate the solid reddish-coloured farms, capped with Roman tiles in ancient style, and frequently placed at the topmost point of this agricultural *oppidum*. It must be said that men return more than adequately their kindly hospitality, greeting them almost systematically with the friendly swaying of a clump of dark cypresses, planted near buildings as if

to call down the blessing of the sun and the heavens upon the birth-pangs of the fertile earth.

When there are several of them, these magnificent hills balance each other and make up a perfectly harmonious landscape, where nothing is grandiose nor formidable, but extremely beautiful, subtle, well-balanced and elegant. The red of the earth, the green of the trees, and the growing crops, the yellow-ochre of the farms, are still further accentuated by the unique quality of the light, famous for its pastel shades, warm with the light, honey-toned highlights, the magic of which has over the centuries won the delight and admiration of painters.

In these dreamlike surroundings, it is not at all surprising that geniuses of all kinds have been able to develop and ripen like fruit, and that round every turning one discovers an old town or some little village, rich in precious reminders of past events; here, in this tiny red-roofed village, Leonardo da Vinci was born; over that other village hovers the memory of Botticelli, and there Catherine of Sienna and Lawrence de Medici came to take the waters; somewhere else Dante chose those feudal towers as the model for the gates of his "Hell"; a little further on it was Machiavelli who dreamed on these shores of his ideal "Prince".

Cradle of the Renaissance, these hills, which gave birth to Pisa, Volterra, Sienna, Florence and so many other famous old towns or anonymous little villages, are the symbol and the very soul of this superb Tuscany, which has enlightened the world with its exquisite art and its humanistic ideas.

In Tuscany, the countryside itself is a pure masterpiece, as can be seen, notably, from the rows of cypress trees at the crest of the hills (below). Right : the hills near San Gimignano.

THE BAY OF NAPLES, VESUVIUS, CAPRI AND ETNA

The sprawling development of the town certainly makes the romantic exclamation of "See Naples and die" somewhat anachronistic. Although the harmonious balance of the lay-out of the gulf is still there, as well as the technicolour blue of the sky and the sea, the proud boast of the tourist brochures, the noise and the dust will drive you to find some other place where you can appreciate to the full the undoubted majestic beauty of the setting.

Let us take Vesuvius first of all. Its legendary outline can be seen from afar, the familiar background on all the postcards. It is a perfect truncated cone in shape, torn open by a succession of terrible eruptions, including the famous one in the year 79 which destroyed the ancient cities of Pompei and Herculaneum, still half buried at its foot.

On the bay, which even the most enthusiastic of superlatives are insufficient to describe, formed as a result of volcanic subsidence during the prehistoric period, the headland of Sorrento lies stretched far out into the sea, like a finger pointing out the Isle of Capri for our admiration. It is there that one must seek the magnetism of the idyllic beauty of the

setting, with which the travellers of the 19th century regaled us so often; Sorrento, standing on the edge of a sheer cliff, overlooking its "marina" built on piles, is a natural rocky balcony, looking over towards Naples, and offering the most outstanding viewpoint from which to survey the famous bay.

On the other side of the headland, the delightful villages built in tiers, Amalfi, Ravello and Positano, clinging to the rocky slopes, are situated one after the other along one of the most scenically beautiful coasts of the Mediterranean, in a tangle of vine arbours, of flowery bowers, or palm-trees and cactuses. As a crowning glory, a small but matchless group of islands extends into the sea the last delightful charms of this well-endowed coastline: Capri, where one discovers side by side memories of mythological tales and the sumptuous well-being of a tourist resort for the wealthy: with as the highlight of the visit the fairylike "Azzurra" grotto, reflecting all the blues of Italy. But there is also the barren island of Ischia, smelling of sulphur and the fish from its little harbours.

Etna, an enormous cone rising up in the centre of Sicily like the big top of an infernal circus putting on diabolical performances, is the backbone, the main attraction and the very heart-beat of the island. The

scars which mark its flanks, the lava flows that swell them, speak eloquently of the torments of its tumultuous history. Although the last of its catastrophic eruptions, which buried Catania, dates back as far as 1669, its activity is more or less permanent. Thus the peacefully wafting white vapour or the thick whirls of black smoke which emanate form the crater at the summit (3,300 metres high) are part of the rhythm of life, and a source of fear, for the villages which are clustered around its foot, drawn there by the fertility of the scoria. Climbing up the side of the volcano leaves unforgettable memories, because of the vastness of the panorama that one discovers, and even more still because of the awesome impression that emanates from this temple to vulcanism; innumerable secondary craters, mounds gaping open in the sides of the mountain, bearing witness to its intense and unpredictable activity.

Left : the famous Faraglioni Rocks, on the island of Capri, and Etna in eruption, striking terror into the hearts of the Sicilians. Right : the Amalfitan coast on the Tyrrhenian Sea and its fairylike atmosphere. Far right, bottom : a view of Positano.

LAKE BLED, PLITVICE AND THE KRKA FALLS, THE FJORDS OF KOTOR

In the heart of Slovenia, the northernmost province of Yugoslavia, recalling Switzerland and Austria, Lake Bled is an international tourist attraction of the first order, deserving superlatives of all kinds and often called "the pearl of the north" by the guides who proudly show it to visitors.

Set in the folds of the Julian Alps, which are a continuation of the Tyrol transformed into the "Triglav national park", massive, imposing mountains of an elegant purity, the lake offers a dignified, yet poetic atmosphere. It is from the ruins of the old feudal castle, dating back to the 11th century, which overlooks the lake and village, that one has the most extensive panorama of the blue of the waters reflecting the circle of blue-green wooded hills that surround the lake, often only vaguely distinguishable in the wisps of mist, which add even more mystery to the already fascinating aura hanging over the area. A charming little romantic road runs round the lake, where Tito used to have a country house on the reed-lined shore. Seeming to float in the middle of the sleeping waters, an island that legend claims was the dwelling-place of Ziva, the Slav goddess of love, is the site for the slender baroque church of St. Mary of the Lake, of which the graceful white silhouette, covered with red tiles, is the only spot of colour standing out on this landscape of differing shades but a monochrome with a base of blues and greens.

The sixteen lakes of Plitvice, some way inland from the Croatian coast, are situated on different levels on the tiered land of a "natural park". They flow into each other, by means of picturesque water-falls, thus forming a chain of small pools, in different shades of blue, with emerald-green highlights, set in an unspoilt environment of steep rocks, the essential charm of this still peaceful and unsophisticated area.

The Krka falls, eighteen kilometres inland from Sibenik, tumble down over a twenty-metre drop with an overpowering thundering noise. A series of natural basins is in perpetual motion, an interesting sight.

The soft limestone rock of which they are composed (calcium carbonate secreted by aquatic mosses) being constantly worn away by erosion.

The beauty of the fjords of Kotor, twisting in and out along the extremely indented coastline, in an overpowering framework of karstic gravelly marl, reaches the height of grandeur because of the absolute desolation of the place. The architect, so it is said, when he planned out the road, made it form the letter M for Milena, the queen of the time, whom he was secretly in love with. However this may be, the winding bends of the maze-like shore, hollowed out into unexpectedly shaped Mediterranean fjords, conceal the magnificent fortified town of Kotor, huddled at the foot of the massive Lovcen, an inhospitable mineral massif, up which runs the famous "ladder" leading to Cetinje, the stark austere capital of the ancient kingdom of Montenegro. A remote, deserted land of wild mountains, yet also an unspoilt area of wonderful lakes, imprisoned in the long yellowish folds of the "Crnagora", the "black mountain".

Yugoslavia. Left : one of the grandiose cascades of the sixteen lakes of Plitvice, and the still waters of Lake Bled. Right : the impressive Mouths of Kotor and one of the fascinating lakes in Montenegro.

MOUNT ATHOS,
THE METEORES AND SANTORIN

On the borders of Turkey, the ancient plain of Thrace, the cradle of the proud and haughty Macedonia, stretches up to the northern gulf of the Aegean Sea through the peninsula of Chalcidicum. A strange headland in the form of a withered hand, dipping its three fingers into the blue waves lapping against the northern Cyclades. The vast beaches running along the two western fingers are new tourist centres and growing seaside resorts, among the most paradisiac in the whole of the Mediterranean.

The most easterly finger is totally different. The pyramid-shaped silhouette of the powerful Mount Athos stands out with its 2,000 metres of sheer rocks rising up above the sea, a formidable petrified ship, moored to the earth by a fragile strand. This inhospitable promontory, feared by ancient navigators, and on which Darius' fleet was dashed to pieces, was chosen by hermits in the tenth century as an ideal spot for fulfilling their desire to withdraw from the world. Amongst them was the famous monk Athanasius, who brought about the success of this "republic of God", and gave his name to the "holy mountain". The fact that it is forbidden to take in "any female being" limits the possibility of discovering all its secrets to the menfolk. This is a pity, for the landscapes are superb and grandiose, with the monasteries perched up high being perfectly integrated into the mountain that they prolong with their contribution of stone.

The same idea of harmonious synergy between man's faith and the mystic impetus of great natural sites, is to be found also when one visits the "Meteores". Between the massifs of Olympus and Pindus, the luxuriant plain of Thessaly, in ancient days the land of the Centaurs, now become the land of swans, used to be flooded by the sea, whose patient toil, gradually eroding the land over a period of a thousand years and more, has cut into the rocky buttresses, leaving gigantic menhirs jutting up from the bottom of the valley of the Peneus, around Trikkala. These imposing peaks, with vertical walls, scarred with cracks and topped with little platforms hanging between earth and sky, appeared in the 14th century to be the ideal refuge for the faithful against the religious persecution being perpetrated by the masters of the Balkans.

So it was that the monasteries of the "Meteores" ("placed on the sky") came to be built, only accessible by means of aerial pulleys or narrow vertiginous staircases, cut into the vertical rock-faces.

Santorin, the "Pearl of the Cyclades", in the far south of the Aegean Sea, facing distant Crete, is the most fantastic of the islands.

Once called "Strongyle" (from *strongylos* which means "pebble") it was at that time a perfectly round hump rising from the waves. In fact, it was the emerging peak of a prehistoric volcano.

One day right back in distant antiquity, it exploded, reducing to powder the cone of its crater, part of which collapsed, allowing the sea to enter. This cataclysm is held to be responsible for the terrifying tidal wave that destroyed the Cretan civilization of Minos, and perhaps engulfed the legendary "Atlantis" of Plato, which is thought to have been situated on this well-favoured, yet ephemeral, island.

The semicircular cliff, 300 metres high, which greets you as you arrive, is a fascinating sight, rather frightening but unforgettable.

In the centre of the bay, the smoking black mound of the present crater, recalls the fragility of man opposed to natural forces.

This outstanding landscape, magnified by the glow of the setting sun, produces in the onlooker a feeling of intense aesthetic and metaphysical emotion.

Greece. Left and below : the amazing peaks of the Meteors with their monasteries seeming to be hanging between heaven and earth. Right : the monastery of Grigoriou on Mount Athos, on the eastern arm of the peninsula of Chalcidicum. Below : a view of the island of Santorin, the "pearl of the Cyclades". Was this, before some great cataclysm, the legendary Atlantis ?

PAMUKKALE, CAPPADOCIA

While the waves of tourists flow on to the beaches and into the resorts of the Turkish coasts all through the year, very few of them go as far as making the exciting discovery of this unforgettable cliff.

On the south buttresses of the Taurus mountains, very near the little town of Denizli, in what was in ancient times Phrygia, on the edge of the kingdom of Pergama, there is to be found an amazing Niagara in stone, dazzling in its whiteness and sparkling in the sun with microscopic little crystalizations. On the barren stony plateau a thermal spring, warm and bubbling, has been spurting up there since very ancient times.

The Romans knew of it and much appreciated it, to such an extent that they established a large settlement there, devoted to the sacred waters called Hierapolis. The spring, dotted with broken ancien columns, is still used as the swimming-pool of a motel. The water which springs from it flows right to the edge of the cliff, where it falls, from basin to basin, on a huge mineral staircase which it has in the course of thousands of years covered with tne sparkling spotless white coat of a chalky deposit, in the same way as our petrifying springs but on the enormous scale of a whole mountain face.

"Pamukkale", the "cotton castle", is a unique sight, congealed waterfalls, where according to legend the Titans came to harvest their cotton. If one allows one's imagination free rein, one can see a piling up of ghostly ramparts with towers grooved with sparkling stalactites. Or some unreal shoal of jellyfish with long veils, solidified by a wicked fairy, while the wonderful chalky dew seeps out in a perpetual oozing, colouring this little piece of cliff with an unintended refinement, turning it into a useless but sublime enchantment.

Right in the heart of Anatolia, at the gates of Kayserie, the barren, desolate high plateau is set in a spectacular subsidence basin: Cappadocia.

The wind and the constant trickling of water have caused a large amount of erosion, forming over the centuries a strange countryside, based on cones topped by a rocky cap which has prevented them from being split like the bare tufa all around. Nowhere else has this phenomenon, referred to by the name of "fairies' chimneys", appeared on such a large scale, or in such perfection. Between Urgup, Avanos and Nevsehir there is simply an amazing number of cones dotted about, raising their proud heads, separated by narrow valleys in which are huddled small villages consisting partly of buildings and partly of cave-dwellings. There too, the strangeness of the natural setting, and the remoteness of its situation, far removed from the rest of the world, made it an ideal haven for persecuted Christians during the period from the 5th to the 19th century. Dwellings, necropolises, churches cut out of the rock, hollowed in the soft tawny-coloured stone, open their empty gaping eyes on the sugar-loafs, without in the least diminishing the effect of their mineral phantasmagoria.

Turkey. Above : the limestone basins of the solidified waterfalls of Pamukkale. Right : overall view of the plain of Cappadocia, in the heart of Anatolia, with its "Fairies' Chimneys", an amazing interweaving of cones sculpted by erosion. Certain of them even contain churches (left).

SINAI AND THE DEAD SEA

The term Sinai designates a triangular peninsula covering an area of 30,000 square kilometres, wedged in between the Red Sea and the Gulf of Akaba. The present Suez canal forms its western boundary, corresponding to the ancient "bitter lakes", the real site for the crossing of the Hebrew people, driven out of Egypt, the place remembered for the Exodus towards the "promised land". A visit to these desert-like valleys thus becomes also a pilgrimage to the holy places of Judeo-Christian tradition.

The jewel of this historically and geographically important area is, of course, Mount Sinai itself, an imposing granite mass, often disturbed by earthquakes, rising up between the Sin desert and the El Qa'ah desert, which stretches as far as Cape Ras Muhamad on the coral-lined shallows of the Charm-el Cheik straits. Several peaks dominate this massif: the Musa jebel (2,050 metres high), where Moses is said to have received the "Tables of the Law": and the Katherina jebel (2,600 metres), at the foot of which stands the famous monastery of St. Catherine, surrounded by its fortified walls in a stony hollow in the desolate plain of I Raha.

The rocky summit, exposed to all the fierce burning heat of the implacable sun, then frozen by the paradoxical cold of nights in the desert, is accessible by means of an incredible staircase consisting of 4,000 steps. This looks down over a never-ending panorama of yellow and brown peaks, torn at by a ruthless perpetually-blowing wind, and coloured by the whims of the ever-moving light, well-suited to rousing a sense of mysticism in the visitors who have ventured to make the exhausting climb. Another dreamlike vision, the oriental charm of the delightful oasis of Feiran, "the pearl of Sinai".

At the foot of the hills of Moab, which turn it into an absolutely desolate closed-in box-like formation, lies the Ghor hollow, the deepest in the world, filled by the Dead Sea, at a level of 392 metres below sea-level. An enormous, unmoving lake, fed only by the river Jordan. The blue-green water, still and heavy, shimmering in the heat, looks like a mercury level, melted in the vaporous setting of the arid, bare mountains that surround the sea. A dead, uncanny landscape. Fish cannot survive in water as salty as this, the level of salinity reaching up to 270 grammes of salt per litre. Nor can plants grow on the shore of the sea, covered with a salty crust formed by the internal evaporation which operates in this mineral melting-pot.

Famous historical sites are hidden around the edge of this diabolical bowl: the rock of Massada and its ruined fortress, glorious scars of the Jewish resistance against the Romans; Quintan, steeped in memories of the Essenes: Sodom and Gomorrha, legendary biblical cities, of which only the site itself and a collection of statues in salt, extraordinary blocks, in which the imagination has difficulty in making out the petrified daughters of Lot; and Petra, the fabulous metropolis of the Nabataeans, clustered together in a unique situation surrounded by high reddish cliffs, hidden in the folds of the Jordanian mountains.

Above : a view of the Dead Sea, near Sodom. Left : Mount Sinaï. Right : aerial view of the Massif of Sinaï, with the famous monastery of St. Catherine.

THE MACKENZIE DELTA
THE BAD LANDS
AND THE ROCKY MOUNTAINS

From the Rocky Mountains to the Arctic, the Canadian Great North is the land of the Mackenzie, a royal river which flows on its way winding its course through the flat northern lands over which hang evanescent mists, and where flaming sunsets burn themselves out. After 4,200 kilometres, the mighty river, having crossed the wonderful landscapes of British Columbia, flows out into the icy Beaufort Sea, through a fabulous delta. Freed from the Franklin and Mackenzie range of hills, and having drained the waters of the Great Slave Lake, the eighth largest in the world, it loses itself as it enters the maze of channels that form the huge estuary where it spreads out its waters. Over an area measuring 210 kilometres in length and 70 metres in width, the wet earth gleams with a glorious display of light, with the backcloth of the aurora borealis and the golden glow of dusk. It is the realm of birds, ducks, swans and wild geese, as well as gulls of all kinds. The Caribou Hills, the only rising land on the bare, desolate tundra, shivering under the onslaught of the Arctic storms, dominate thousands of irregular gullies, feeling their way through the sodden sandbanks.

A hundred million years ago, other prehistoric monsters lived in the foothills of the Rocky Mountains, on the ridge of the legendary "prairie". The Red Deer has patiently hollowed out a valley, one kilometre wide and 320 kilometres long, within the base of the soft, crumbly rocks that make up the substratum of this region of Alberta. The geological variety of these lands explains the polychrome aspect, dazzling and unexpected, of this strange technicolour scar, interrupting the flat monotony of the endless wheat plains. The bright kaleidoscope of these Bad Lands is a pleasant transition leading to the nearby mighty domain of the Rocky Mountains. Certainly only a small part of this overpowering range, reaching from Arctic Alaska to the hard-baked shores of the gulf of lower California, lies within Canadian territory, but the most beautiful natural sites are grouped together here, offering tourist

attractions of the first order. The hot-water springs (40°) of Rabbitkettle in the grandiose setting of a broad valley cut by impressive gorges, stream down a giant-sized staircase made of basins one on top of the other, petrifying through limestone with yellowish oxydations the steps of this geological amphitheatre, which recalls the Turkish cliff of Pamukkale.

The Fraser canyon, a tormented mineral gorge, seems to torture, kilometre after kilometre, a turbulent, roaring river, imprisoned within vertiginously high and spectacular walls. The glacier of Mount Columbia, an immense and superb icefield, covering 300 km², set between the bare facets of a crown of peaks reaching a height of more than 3,700 metres, is the residue from a glacial cap which used to cover Canada in prehistoric times. It recedes 30 metres a year, but still remains impressive.

Canada. Left, top : the Mauricia. Above : aerial view of the huge delta of the Mackenzie river, in the territories of the north-west of the country. Left : Fraser canyon. Right : the Badlands, home of the Red Deer, in Alberta.

more spectacular. They throw up a cloud of spray, sprinkling the whole area around with fine drops of water, and permanently producing wonderful rainbows.

The continuation of the Rocky Mountains, the Alaska range, a formidable barrier which rises between the shores of the Pacific and the frozen "Prairies" of the Canadian Great North. This powerful granite massif reaches a height of 6,190 metres with Mount Mackinley, the roof of the North American continent. In spite of its enormous mass, it is an elegant, stately mountain, reigning over a wild, desolate world, a unique glacial environment, resulting from the quatenary glaciations. Rich in metal-bearing lodes, especially veins of gold, the valleys which groove its base were the scene of the invasion of gold-diggers searching for nuggets in the gold-rush of the middle of the 19th century. And it was two gold-seekers who, in 1910, achieved the first ascent of its immaculate dome.

From high up there, one can look down on the diaphanous, sparkling world of the great glaciers that encircle the topmost crests, in the shadow of the Muldrow, the finest and the most eye-catching, with its immense icefield, covering 500 km² and stretching its long tongue out over a distance of more than 60 km. Its upper basin is enclosed by an amphitheatre of reddish rocks, striated as if by claw-marks with an infinite number of little channels, where the slope is such that the snow cannot take hold. and limits itself to outlining prettily the topmost ridges. Advancing about 50 metres a year, it sometimes happens during the period of "surge" (flood) that it exceeds 300 metres per day!

THE NIAGARA FALLS
MOUNT MACKINLEY

Astride the frontier between Canada and the United States, the region of the Great Lakes is a fine illustration of geological history. The rocky "shield" of the Canadian North, laid bare during the thawing of the ice, has revealed profound, closed-in valleys, scars of the ancient moraines. Filled up with the constantly streaming water, and being badly drained, they give rise to lakes. In the order of their geographical progression, one finds Lake Superior, the largest of all (covering 80,000 km²) and the deepest (430 metres); Lake Huron, Lake Michigan, penetrating deeply into American territory, reaching as far as Detroit and Chicago; the little Lake Erie, and Lake Ontario, on the last step, opening out on to the plain. The famous Niagara Falls lie between Lake Erie and Lake Ontario. Formerly surrounded by a dense forest, which has now disappeared.

If for the purists, the Niagara Falls are not the most beautiful in the world, they are certainly the most famous and the most easily accessible: three million visitors come here every year, to admire the breathtaking sight they offer. They were created as the result of a difference in geological texture between the hard rocks of the high plateaus upstream, which resisted erosion better than those downstream, which have gradually crumbled and been worn away. The result has been, over thousands of years, the formation of a kind of "sill", forcing the water to pass from a height of 170 metres to a lower level of 75 metres, between the two lakes, the cataracts, as such, representing a difference in level of a straight fall of 50 metres.

There are, in fact, two waterfalls; the smaller (330 metres wide) in American territory, the larger (660 metres wide) and the more beautiful, on Canadian soil. These falls, called "the horseshoe" because of their curved, semi-circular shape, are the

Above and right : two photos of the Niagara Falls, the most famous falls in the world. Below : Mount MacKinley, the "roof" of the North-American continent. Its highest point reaches 6 190 metres.

THE BADLANDS OF SOUTH DAKOTA
MONUMENT VALLEY
THE GRAND CANYON OF COLORADO

In South Dakota, the strip of the Badlands, stretching along at the foot of the Rocky Mountains, offers a strange landscape of crossing ravines, lofty spurs and jagged needle-like points, cut out of a crumbly ocre tuff. It required 35 millions years to raise this prehistoric lake bottom, made up of clays and alluvium in successive layers, an ideal terrain for erosion by water and wind to work on, sculpting a petrified forest, in amazing shapes and warm shades of colour. On the road taken by the long caravans of pioneer coaches going west, other reliefs, unusual and photogenic, are to be seen at intervals, on the edge of the vast, almost endless plains of the Middle West: the strange Chimney Rock, a rocky point, 46 metres high, set aloft on a cone of scree, which used to be used as a landmark on this plain of semi-desert. Further south, the surprising Devil's Tower, a striking jet of lava, cooled and set on the spot, reaches a height of 265 metres above the rolling undulation of grass-covered hills.

Cutting through the desert substratum of Colorado, runs the amazing wooded canyon of "Mesa Verde", whose gigantic yellowish overhanging projections were the shelter chosen by the Indian nomads. The other sites in the province are striking in their desolation and their stark barrenness. The most famous of these landscapes is "Monument Valley", which has been used as the setting for so many Westerns.

Right in the heart of the country of the Navajos Indians, the centre of the present high plateau of Colorado (from 1,600 to 2,300 metres in altitude) was the bottom of an arm of the sea, running in from the Gulf of Mexico seventy million years ago. When the sea withdrew, it left a layer of unstable sedimentary land that erosion has since that time worn down, levelled and destroyed completely, with the exception of superb tabular debris, oversized pillars of a huge imaginary edifice, ghosts of crumbling fortresses. Their pink and yellowish mass, enormous and overpowering, dominate from a height of 300 to 600 metres the desolate plain, which the wind powders with reddish-coloured sand.

It was in a neighbouring region that one of the largest known meteorites chose to land. when it was hurled down to earth, in the heart of Arizona. This is such a barren zone that the crater of its impact was only discovered in 1871. Yet the hole was enormous; 1,300 metres in diameter and 180 metres deep, with raised edges of 50 metres. It has been calculated that this meant that it must have been a meteor weighing two million tons, travelling at a speed of 10 kilometres per second!

Another surprise awaits you when you discover the unique view offered by the Grand Canyon of Colorado, perhaps the most outstanding and breathtaking natural wonder on our planet. As soon as one sets eyes on it for the first time, one is struck, then overwhelmed and fascinated by this symphony of lines, volumes and colours. The horizontal strata. which make up the structure of the canyon, are like the lines of a musical score, on which are written the coloured notes of which this hymn to beauty is composed.

The luxuriance, the variety and the richness of the landscapes, looked down on from the roads and belvederes which are to be found from time to time along the two banks, make all descriptions sound lyrical and call for superlatives of all kinds.

Some 100 million years ago, this area was simply a barren plateau, composed of sedimentary strata resting on the granite shield of the continental shelf. The ebb and flow of the sea, covering and gradually hollowing out the gorge that we can admire today, and the nearby canyons, formed the present landscape over the years. The magnificent stratified layers which stripe the sloping banks at the bottom of which the torrent seethes, are a geology lesson in themselves. A stratigraphic study of them reveals the tectonic history of this part of the world. They also prove the power of the natural forces involved and the patient tenacity of the processes that have formed our world.

U.S.A. Above : a strange sight of the Badlands, in South Dakota. Right : the rocky points of Monument Valley, on the high plateau of Colorado. Below : a striking impression of the Grand Canyon in Colorado, taken from one of the numerous belvederes on the perimeter.

THE PARK OF ARCHES
GUNNISON'S BLACK CANYON
BRICE CANYON

The Park of Arches is another landmark in Utah. Its originality lies in the shapes that erosion has formed out of a base of red sandstone. The name itself is significant, a reminder of those ruiniform structures, dominated by arches, sturdy or elegant, solid or slender, which span ghostly obstacles. The "Landscape Arch", a delicate basket-handle of sandstone, 100 metres long, is the most perfect masterpiece of this imaginary, dreamlike architecture.

Two other canyons complete the store of riches of this part of the West: "Gunnison's Black Canyon" cuts through the peaceful plateau of colorado over a distance of 16 kilometres and is often as much as 600 metres high. It needed two million years to bring this process to its climax, and in particular to brighten with large white bands, formed by the agglutination of a multitude of feldspar crystals, the gloomy dark cliffs, inhospitable and closed in on upon each other along this rugged rift valley.

"Brice Canyon" does not really deserve the name of "canyon", for it is not a deep enclosed valley but the versant of a plateau, exposed to wind and water, which has gradually disintegrated. The originality and the beauty of the region depend on the colours of its clay and sandstone ruins, varying from orange to bright or garnet red. The resemblance of the shapes to amassed colonades and architectural debris, is such that the imagination leaps through this odd mass of rubble, recognizing here and there a face, discovering the wall of some monumental ruins. They are sedimentary lacustrian rocks, which, over a distance of two kilometres and a width of 600 metres, make up the tender delicate soul of this outstanding "Pink Cliff", with its delightfully elegant sculptures and its fairylike effects of light.

U.S.A. The incredible sights of Utah. Above : the "Dead Horse Point". Below : one of the numerous natural arches in the Park of Arches. Opposite : an aerial view, which allows one to appreciate to the full the beauty and richness of the formations of Brice Canyon. Far right : the rocks of Cedar Breaks.

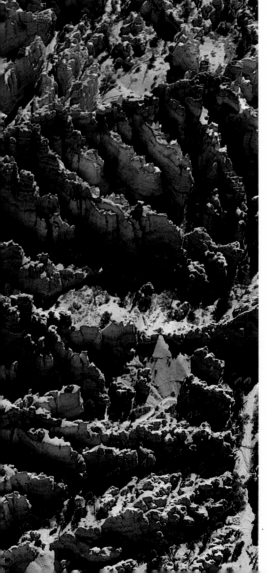

YELLOWSTONE PARK

To the north-west of Wyoming, Yellowstone Park, the oldest established national park in the U.S.A., is situated at an altitude of 2,500 metres, in the centre of the Rocky Mountains, where it spreads far and wide its marvellous and diabolical kingdom.

A real geological treat, it can offer a whole arsenal of the most spectacular phenomena ever produced on the earth's crust. This explains the profusion and the richness of the sites to be discovered along the whole length of the 250 kilometres of the superb panoramic road that runs through the park. Two hundred geysers, some of them spouting regularly, some only intermittently, put on a magnificent show, discharging at a height of from 2 to 100 metres their gushing jets, while other mouths of hell pour forth waves of hot water, steaming and bubbling, from a multitude of mineral springs, loaded with salts colouring or petrifying the rocks.

Under the pure luminous sky of Wyoming, one can discover the most popular attractions beloved by tourists: vast moraines, dotted with gigantic erratic blocks, the result of the great glaciations; valleys with their slopes eroded, cut by canyons and gorges; fossilized, petrified forests, close to the skeletons of mammoths, which bear witness to the immense extent of the naturalistic past of these high lands. The result is an incredible density of outstanding, extraordinary landscapes, where some "three-star" sites top the bill: the canyon of Yellowstone river, which owes its name to the dazzlingly bright yellow rock forming its walls; the massif of the great Teat (4,190 metres), an overpowering mass of granite, set amongst lakes, forests and glaciers which give it a striking Alpine look; the "Moon Craters", a cluster of multicoloured lava mounds, looking like swellings in a vast field of scoria, charred remains of an intense, recent vulcanism, resulting in a lunar-type landscape, where one can discover every imaginable

type of volcano; the Snake River, which, after a majestic stretch running through a grandiose setting of high valleys, hollows out a series of amazing canyons in the limestone rocks, transforming them into sensational gorges, the deepest in the U.S.A. (2,400 metres of sheer cliff).

U.S.A. Top, left, opposite and below : the spectacular multicolour basins of the natural park of Yellowstone Park, in Wyoming. Left, bottom : the water of this waterfall in the park, warm and extremely rich in lime, has created terraces of white basins. Above : the Snake River, at the foot of Mount Moran, in the Great Teat Park. Far right : "Spider Rock" in the Chelly Canyon, in Arizona.

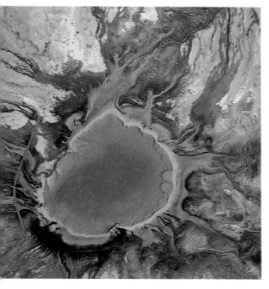

DEATH VALLEY AND YOSEMITE PARK

The Colorado plateau is flanked by two well-defined desert-like depressions, but nonetheless, impressive and spectacular.

The more famous of the two is Death Valley, a popular tourist attraction in California. A simple hollow, 200 kilometres long, and between five and twenty metres wide, the bare mountains that surround it transform this bowl into a furnace. The bottom of it, at a depth of 86 metres below sea-level, is filled by a small brackish lake, which never dries up completely, in spite of the evaporation and the burning heat, which can reach a temperature of 57°. It well deserves its name of "Badwater", for the high level of salt produces total desolation, heightened even further by the salt desert that occupies the adjacent plain, having taken the place of the ancient prehistoric lake. This extended over a much larger area and served as a slide for the huge erratic blocks pushed by the wind across this geological glacis.

Like the luxuriant California itself, overflowing with riches, Yosemite Park is a museum of all that is extraordinary and gigantic. Everything is "bigger and better" than elsewhere: the "Captain" massif, mountainous ossature of this micro-region, is more imposing, with its 745 metres; the falls that pound down into the river Yosemite are higher than the

Niagara Falls; the famous "mirror-lake" is more limpid and reflects more than any other lake, reflecting the lofty peaks that surround it in its most pure waters; its forest of sequoias are the finest and contain the tallest trees (the "Grizzly" that measures 65 metres); not to mention the glacier and the striking Merced Canyon, among the most fascinating on the North American Continent.

Compared with the wonderful West, which jealously hoards all the great natural sites, the East has not a great deal to offer, except the pleasant, majestic beauties of the gigantic basin of the Missouri and the Mississippi. However, the Florida Marshes, totally different from the grandiose desolate landscapes, are wonderful, even unique, areas to discover. Everything combines to perfection, the tropical climate, the dimension, the flora and the fauna, to glorify this area, a paradise of lake and other watery landscapes. The marshes cover the south of the Florida peninsula.

U.S.A. Left-hand page : in the Valley of Yosemite, in California, flows the Marcde. Below : the salt lake of Badwater, with the Panamint Mountains, in the famous "Death Valley", also in California. Above : the Cypress Gardens in Florida. Left : one of the gigantic trees in the Sequoia National Park.

ACAPULCO BAY, POPOCATEPETL AND THE CANYONS OF THE TARAHUMARA

As famous as the bay of Naples, Acapulco Bay is one of the high spots of international tourism and the most famous seaside resort in Mexico. It is true that its rough rocks provide it with a unique situation on

necessary for the preparation of powder. They found up there a crater containing a lake bubbling with molten magma. Today the mouth of the volcano is blocked up by a cone of solidified lava and contents itself with discharging harmless exhalations. The last eruption dates back as far as the 18th century: this ultimate effort did not prevent the "volcaneros",

the Mexican coast, which is otherwise completely flat and sandy all the way down. It was formed, in the Tertiary period, by the brutal and chaotic collapse of the Sierra Madre into the Pacific. This has resulted in a succession of little creeks and high cliffs scalloping the shoreline of the headland, which makes up the most important part of the area. The attraction of the "Aztec Jump", performed by daring youngsters, the "clavadores", consists of diving into the blue waters of these creeks from the top of impressive rock faces, about 20 metres high and some five metres only from the level of the water. The most spectacular and the narrowest is Quebrada.

The main road linking Mexico City and Puebla passes through the solid buttresses of the Sierra Nevada and offers at one viewpoint an imposing silhouette of Popocatepetl. With its perfectly-shaped cone, everlastingly covered with snow, the volcano always seems to stand proudly aloft. Even if it no longer justifies its name of "smoking mountain", its 5,452 metres and the purity of its lines continue to arouse admiration and still encourage many travellers to attempt to climb it, a not very difficult undertaking. I wonder if they know that Cortes' conquistadors were the first to make the climb and reach the top. They did it for two reasons; first to subjugate the Aztecs, for whom the mountain was sacred, and secondly to bring back the sulphur

however, from continuing to exploit the sulphur right up to 1920. From the dazzling white ice-cap which tops the sleeping giant, the panorama covers a huge area, looking out over the Mexican high plateau and the nearby volcano, Ixtacciuatl.

Little known and difficult to reach, the folds of the Sierra Madre, which form the territory of the Tarahumara Indians, offer the finest landscapes in Mexico. They originated through the erosion of the rocks by the water trickling down them, thus carving out hollows and ravines in the high plateaus and cutting the rock into thousands of gorges, called the "Barrancas", often more than 50 kilometres long and several hundred metres high, and they hide within them the raging torrent of a "rio", imprisoned between their sheer, steep walls of rock. No road goes anywhere near here, and only the railway linking Clulmahua to the Pacific allows the visitor to catch an unforgettable glimpse of the panorama, from belvederes that have been strategically placed above the most spectacular spots: the fantastic "barranca del cobre" and the gorge of the rio Urique, which is really a sensational sight.

Mexico. Above : the famous Popocatepetl (in the Aztec language this means "smoking mountain"). Right : the extraordinary setting of the Bay of Acapulco. Below : the strange beauty of Lake Pazcuaro.

JAMAICA

Jamaica, with Cuba and Haiti, forms part of the Greater Antilles, spreading its garland of enchantment in the warm sweetly-perfumed Caribbean Sea. 240 kilometres by 85, a dense relief produced by a tertiary fold, reaching a height of 2,500 metres, it bathes in a tropical climate, caressed by the trade-winds, but also frequently buffeted by the force of terrifying cyclones. A land of both blessings and excesses. The fact is that there has been an artificial mixture of two opposite worlds on these dream islands, since Christopher Columbus landed there in 1492. The introduction of African slaves during the sixteenth century brought in the brutal sorcery of Africa and the pleasant languour of Indian autochtons, which were gradually destroyed over the years.

A visit to the island offers the possibility of discovering superb landscapes, also of very contrasting varieties; the shores are delightful.

To the east, the "blue mountains" are covered with dense forests, brightened by the dazzling colour of thousands of orchids. In the centre and towards the west, the vast limestone plateau has been tortured by 140 million years of erosion, to become a fantastic karstic universe, worn, chiselled and twisted. This is the region of the famous "Cockpits", by

analogy with the little arenas where the cock-fights are organized. The surface of the rock is hollowed out into "dolines", hemispherical hollows, carpeted with luxuriant vegetation, which were traditionally used as a refuge for the native inhabitants on the various occasions that colonizing invaders arrived. Now, it is the tourists who have taken possession of the island. They cluster together around Montego Bay, close to the beach where Columbus landed, and radiate from there along the "Cockpit" quays. A trip down the rapids of the Rio Grande on a raft must be fitted into one's programme, as well as a visit to the caves with the "pearl-covered" floor, "pearls" that are in fact millions of little snail shells petrified in a thin layer of limestone. Another sight not to be missed is the strange "Hellshire" mountains, worn away by the scars inflicted on them by erosion, and where nothing else grows except bristling but superb cactuses. Yet no reference to hell or to the devil can make the tourist forget his happiness at finding himself here on this paradise. He does not really know how nearly right he is, since Jamaica is one of the sites suggested as the possible location for the Biblical earthly paradise.

Jamaica. Above : the bay of Port Antonia. Far left : a sight of the famous Montego Bay. Opposite : the Ocho Rio Falls, one of the jewels of this tourists' paradise.

THE VALLEY OF MACHU PICHU
LAKE TITICACA, ALTIPLANO
AND THE GREAT CORDILLERA

Quite apart from the exceptional archaeological interest of the Inca ruins crowning its peaks, the high valley of the rio Urubamba, whose turbulent waters eventually pour out into the Amazon basin, is a naturally grandiose site; perhaps the most remarkable in the whole of Peru.

A narrow, perilously-perched railway line winds its way along the side of the mountain, in amongst the tiered terraces clinging to the slightest sign of a ledge on the steep rock-faces. The valley of Vilcanota, beyond Pisac, is the most spectacular stretch of this aerial "Inca road", crawling along amongst the buttresses of the cordillera, between rugged peaks, steep promontories, and tiny little orchards, alternating on the "andenes" (terraces) with a few miserable acres of maize.

The great attraction of Peru, however, is the magnificent Lake Titicaca, a vast stretch of blue on a backcloth of eternal snow. The highest (3,812 metres) and the most extensive (6,900 km²) network of navigable waterways in the world, it is not only a geographical entity, but also a cultural symbol and, indisputably, a natural wonder. In spite of its relative shallowness (it is 280 metres deep), the mass of water there is such that its temperature remains steadily at about 11°, even producing a gentle climate on its shores. An enormous lake, unique, with hidden secrets, in the heart of the central Andes mountains, whose snow-covered summits guarantee the most sumptuous of backgrounds.

Thus, situated partly in Peru and partly in Bolivia, the lake occupies the centre of the "Altiplano", a barren and arid high plateau, stretching out at an altitude of 4,000 metres, swept by the icy winds that come swirling down from the lonely, desert-like frozen wastes of the nearby cordillera. For it is, in fact, at this level that the Andes are the most accessible. This well-known name, which fascinates us and rouses our imagination, belongs to the longest mountain range in the world, stretching over a distance of 1,000 kilometres along the west coast of South America, right down to Cape Horn. A complex intrication of massifs over 6,000 metres high, it can only be explored with great difficulty, and nobody has forgotten the obstacle that it represented for the heroic setting up of the air routes for transporting mail.

But this gigantic jagged barrier, indented like a dinosaur's backbone, spreads out towards the north and softens its slopes to form the "Altiplano", an icy, desolate high plateau, which extends towards the heart of Bolivia, the roof of South America, surrounded, as if imprisoned, by the Andes. The road to La Paz runs through the majestic setting of this fairylike kingdom of eternal snow, the refuge of the Inca gods, that this magnificent white cordillera, or "Real", represents, dominated by its two superb jewels, the Illampu and the Illimani (6,160 metres) "the dazzling falcons" of Indian mythology, with such frighteningly steep slopes that chaotic glaciers are forced to release their seracs because they cannot hold them on the vertical rock-faces.

Above : the mountain of Illimani, near La Paz, in Bolivia, which reaches a height of 6 460 metres. Below : a view of the valley of Las Ancimas ("of souls") and the Cordillera Blanca, in Peru. Right, top : the extraordinary blue colour of Lake Titicaca, on a background made up of snowcovered mountains. Opposite : a view of the Altiplano, a high desert plateau of the Andes.

SALTO DEL ANGEL, THE BAY OF RIO AND THE IGUACU FALLS

It is in the Guianese province that the natural beauties of Venezuela are to be found, and especially in the sandstone massif of the Rotaima (2,900 metres), through which flows the river Carrao, an affluent of the much larger and stronger-flowing Oronoco. A first group of waterfalls, the turbulent, foaming Canaima Falls, offer a breathtaking sight to the tourists of the region. But it is a good deal further on that one must go to discover the "Salto del Angel", the highest waterfall in the world. As the journey there takes five days in a motor-driven canoe, the only comfortable way to visit the falls is to fly over them; the aerial view of the falls seen from the plane is an unforgettable experience. It is strange to think that it is the same river Carrao, now calm and flowing peacefully on its way, that, before crossing the high wooded plateau of the Auvan Tepui, runs over the karstic ledge and disappears into a steep crevasse in this tabular massif. The small amount of water in the river only allows it to form one single cascade, but it streams rapidly down like a blade, cutting through the green coat of the forest and the tawny drapes of the cliff, in a clear drop in a straight line, before crashing down to 1,000 metres lower down.

Whether you arrive by boat or by plane, the famous Bay of Rio offers itself to you, wide open to receive your admiration at the very first sight of it. Over 360°, sea and mountains provide this unique setting, unequalled anywhere in the world, supplying to your wondering eyes the best-known elements to be found on postcards. It was in 1502 that the Portuguese caravels of Pedro Cabral came to land in this superb harbour to which they gave the name of Rio de Janeiro, "the river of January", having wrongly taken it to be the estuary of a river. This accidental masterpiece of nature consists of the collapsed debris of a coastal range of mountains in wooded tiers with narrow alluvial plains, edged by a series of dazzling crescents of sand. The two most famous of these beaches, whose very names set us dreaming, are Flamengo and Copacabana, forming a 6-kilometre-long border to the vast bay of Guanabara.

Within the embrace of its perfect curve, the bay holds a number of little islands and submerged rocks, forgotten by the erosion to the advance posts of the coast, and which rise up like petrified sentries at their posts.

These "Moros" are the remains of the original granite shelf, stripped and laid bare by the oxidation of the soft rocks on the surface which cannot resist the wearing away that is rapid in this tropical climate. They are all familiar these dome-shaped rocks, covered with curious curved slabs of stone and with a sparse close-cropped vegetation: the "Corcovado" or "Hunchback", which, since 1931, has borne the giant statue of Christ by Landowski; the

Brazil. Above : a view of Amazonia. Right : the bay of Rio de Janeiro, and the famous Sugarloaf Mountain.

"Morro da Urca": and most important of all, the famous "Sugar Loaf" a superb cone of pure rock, sheer vertically and bare, which has now become the sign and the symbol of the "Belacap" (beautiful capital), the city called by the Brazilians themselves, with emotion and admiration, the "Ciudade Maravillosa", the marvellous city.

On the border between Brazil and Argentina, in the surroundings of the luxuriant vegetation of the tropical basin of the huge Parana river, are hidden some incredible cataracts. Higher, more extensive and more abundant than the Niagara Falls, they shed by means of their numerous falls, one beside the other and as high as 60 to 80 metres, the slack waters of the oversized river at the bottom of a vast canyon in the shape of an arc, a bubbling and tumultuous channel. A deafening thundery noise accompanies the undulation of the moving liquid curtains, adorning the green girdle of the forest with their vaporous drapery. Although they are accessible from Argentina, it is from the Brazilian side that the beauty of the setting can best be appreciated. It is also possible to draw nearer to them by means of a network of vertiginous footbridges. It is from these that one can see that thousands of exotic birds and a host of beautiful multicoloured butterflies hover amongst the clumps of scraggy vegetation which struggle to survive between the different stretches of water.

And one can better understand the remake made by the somewhat disillusioned President Roosevelt after a visit he made to this watery fairyland. He simply said: "Poor Niagara"!

Above : an aerial view of the Amazon, near Manaus. Right : two photos of the tropical forest of Amazonia. Below : the breathtaking waterfalls of the Iguacu, on the frontier between Brazil and Argentina.

ACONCAGUA, THE VALLEY OF THE LUNA, THE REGION OF THE CHILIAN LAKES, PUNTA ARENAS AND CAPE HORN

Argentina is the proud possessor of the most beautiful and the least-known landscapes in the whole of Latin America, dotted about on the edge of the mythical "Pampa". Apart from the grandiose Iguacu Falls, shared with Brazil, the most beautiful spots are concentrated around Mendoza, in the central cordillera, and at the most extreme point of the Andes of Patagonia.

The menacing Aconcagua, the highest point of the Andes (6,960 metres high) dominates part of the cordillera, which is exceptionally dry and desolate. This adds a harshness and a grandeur to the landscape that is still further accentuated by the incredible sheerness of its slopes, where the snow has difficulty in finding a hold and seems to fray away into long swathes, which are blown about by the gusts of the famous "white wind", as it sweeps across this "roof of the Andes" at 150 kilometres an hour. It is through this mighty massif that the highest road in the world threads its way, linking Buenos Aires to Valparaiso, in a hieratic and frighteningly immense world.

Nearby, the Titanic chaos, permanently frozen by petrifying waters, and known under the name of the "bridge of the Inca" is a gigantic archway, 50 metres long and 15 metres wide, spanning the Rio de Cuevas which flows down with its tumultuous, chalky waters forty metres below.

Set in the folds of the Sierra de Cordoba, the famous "Valley of the Luna" corresponds to the bottom of a prehistoric lake, now dried out. Over its 1,750 m², intense erosion has worn away the volcanic rocks, the sandstone and strange-coloured tuffs, rich in all the colours of the rainbow from the oxydation of the rocks and full of fossils. The result is an apocalyptic landscape, both desolate and fascinating at the same time, a mineral phantasm in technicolour, disturbing yet superb.

Nor does the Chilian side let itself lag behind. To the south of Valdivia, the region of the lakes, called "The Garden of the Gods", is a mosaic of twenty-five huge stretches of blue water (from 15 to 900 square kilometres in area) in which are reflected the snow-covered and sometimes smoking cones of the numerous volcanos. The emerald-green sheet of water called the "Todos los Santos", is a lake that gathers the icy waters of the powerful Tronador and vies in beauty with the immaculate pyramid of the volcano Osorno, playing in the opalescent waves of the Llanquihue. Faced with such vast and grandiose scenery, one cannot help thinking of Canada and all that the Rocky Mountains can offer.

On the other hand, the crumbling away of the extreme point of the cordillera, to the south of Puerto Montt, has left a unique headland, strange and haunting, only accessible by boat. Constantly buffeted by storms, these southerly rocks, seemingly at the end of the world, form a whole universe of giant canals and fjords, through which run the famous Magellan Straits. Punta Arenas is the capital of the whole of this confused area, composed of foaming ocean, lifelessterritory, mad wind and the dominating icy wastes. an archipelago of jagged mountains, in fantastic shapes, of which the "Torre del Paine" is one of the most spectacular and unusual, emerges from a blanket of mist to reveal the very last of them, the almost frightening silhouette of the legendary Cap Horn, the mythological end of the world.

Patagonia. Above : Lake Azul and the striking chain of the Torres del Paine. Right : two views of the very varied landscapes to be found in Patagonia.

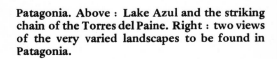

MOUNT MAYON, MAUNA LOA, MOOREA, BORA BORA

The Pacific Ocean is dotted with a multitude of islands, isolated or grouped together in archipelagos, some of them of some importance, others simply a volcanic peak rising out of the sea. They all share one thing in common, the intense blue of the sky and the sea, a dazzling border of white sand, with, scattered here and there, languorous coconut palms and a series of lagoons with sparkling bluey-green, turquoise and emerald highlights, sheltered within the embrace of coral reefs.

This means that the least little island seems like heaven. However, this world of wonders has its high places, which possess all these beauties to a superlative degree. In the Philippines, it is the Mayon, another formidable volcano, whose cone, as perfect as a geometrical drawing, has been quietly smoking in the trade-winds since its last angry outburst in 1897, at the edge of the straits of San Bernadino, for which it serves as a landmark, standing out like a monumental Indian tent.

Hawaii, although synonymous with laziness and a peaceful, unhurried existence, possesses, among a host of extinct volcanos, the imposing Mauna Loa, one of the most active in the world. It reaches a height of 4,170 metres, standing on the ocean bed, which is 5,000 metres deep at this point; this represents a tremendous mass of lava, piled up to a height of over 9,000 metres, higher than Mount Everest and, in volume, five times as big as Mount Fuji! If one adds to all this the fact that it is extremely active still, and has overflowed in eruption about forty times in the last hundred years, it can be

seen that it really is the greatest producer of lava in the world.

The Polynesian islands, although also due to volcanic activity, offer views and impressions that are fortunately more peaceful and serene.

Moorea, the twin sister of the overcrowded Tahiti, is an outstanding example of the remodelling of an old volcanic structure over a period of thousands of years. Under the protection of a barrier reef, creating a delightful lagoon with opaline tints, basalt peaks and cliffs in fantastic jagged shapes, hide their brown rocks under a blanket of white sand, made up of immaculate coral dust, crushed to powder by erosion.

The Bora Bora rock is on a much smaller scale, and still more schematic in its representation of Polynesian nature: on its surface of 8 km by 5 it has gathered together all that goes to make up the attraction of these well-favoured islands: a scattering of little islands, scalloped with deep crescent-shaped bays, with a crest of swaying coconut palms, steep peaks raising their dark basalt flanks high above the thick green carpet of tropical vegetation. The aerial

The islands of Hawaii do not only have dream-like beaches to offer, like this one, Lumahai Beach at Kauai (right), but also some almost moonlike landscapes, like the canyon of Waimea (below).

view from a flight over Bora Bora is unforgettable. In a single glance, one can appreciate all the characteristic beauty of the island and let oneself be carried away by the splendour of its encircling turquoise waters, a pictorial image of a halo of coral reefs, protecting the pale lagoon and its bright emerald-lined beaches with formidable ramparts on which the waves, driven in by the fury of the ocean, pound with all their might.

Polynesia. Above : one of the enchanting bays of the island of Moorea, Cook's Bay. Left : the waters of the lagoon of Papetoai, on Moorea, which surprise us with their perfect transparency. Right : an aerial view of Raititi Point, at Bora-Bora, their impressive rocks of basalt contrasting strongly with the gentle waters of the azure-blue sea.

THE ATOLLS

Another magic word, synonymous with fairyland, escape from one's normal surroundings, and perfect beauty. It represents part of our mythological heritage and our store of dreams.

However, the Atoll, before being the object of dreams and admiration, was the result of very special geo-biological circumstances. At its origin, one finds one of the innumerable volcanic cones hardly emerging from the sea, still covered by a metre or two of water. On the immersed slopes, colonies of madrepores cling and spread, living multicoloured coral, which die off leaving behind their skeleton of which limestone, whose wearing away in erosion produces the immaculate sand that makes up the substance and the coastal edge of the future island. Stretching between this circular crown of coral and the shores of the island lies the girdle of the lagoon. The shallowness of its waters guarantees its superb opalescent shades of colour, from jade to emerald. The sea there, protected by the barrier of the coral reef, through which only one or two breaches allow access, is exceptionally warm and calm.

What produces the unreal beauty of the atolls is the palette of colours with which they are painted, ranging from the deep blue of the sea to the velvety green of the palm-trees, with the graduating shades of the lagoon and the bright whiteness of the strip along the coral-dust beaches. This same combination exists everywhere where there are colonies of constructive polyparies. Their presence is extremely important, vital in fact, since it is fundamental in the formation of coral reefs, and so of atolls. Whithout coral there would have been none of those little islands, bristling with coconut-trees, which are so common in the Pacific and the Indian Ocean.

The most beautiful of the atolls are dotted about in these two oceans. The archipelago of the Maldives, with a total of about 2,000 islands scattered over an area of 300 km², has about twenty that are really outstanding. The same can be said of Micronesia, which is another treasure-house containing similar jewels, but it takes much longer to reach and the journey is difficult. Who does not remember the famous island of Bikini, where man tried to improve on the original polychrome beauty by adding his own diabolical atom shows. The coral sea, so rightly named, contains others gathered around New Caledonia, fine specimens these. Lastly, it is in French Polynesia that one can most easily acquaint oneself with the atolls. Moorea, and even more important, Bora-Bora, are the highlights of this tour of discovery, though it must be admitted that it is from the air that the sight is the most amazing. This is the only way to be able to appreciate the general overall view of this fascinating green and white "raft", floating on the infinite expanse of azure blue, an azure that reigns supreme over both sea and sky.

Above : landscapes in Moorea and Tahiti. Left : two atolls. Below : the island of Pines, in New Caledonia.

THE SIMPSON DESERT,
THE BLUE MOUNTAINS,
THE CLIFFS OF PORT CAMPBELL

Australia, which represents more than one fifth of the earth's land surface, is the flattest and driest country in the world. Three-quarters of it is made up of a desert-like plateau without any real river, and dotted with the debris of the oldest mountains on earth. Right in the centre, the Simpson Desert contains the highlights of a tour of age-old Australia.

It is there, near Alice Springs, that one can most easily penetrate into this wonderful prehistoric region. Over an area of 300,000 km², this desert of red sand extends its tawny dunes, bristling with thorny bushes, as far as the vast depression of Lake Eyre, an immense and rather strange stretch of brackish water, which decreases in size every year, since the rainfall does not reach more than 130 mm compared with a record evaporation level of 2 m! Along the edge of this desolate expanse of water, can be seen at intervals of some tens of kilometres the remains of the most ancient and the most extraordinary mountains that are to be seen on earth.

The MacDonnel Mountains, thought to be 400 million years old, are remarkable for their odd shape, with long striated bands, looking like an old comb with broken teeth. No higher than 1,200 metres in altitude, they are a fascinating sight, especially because of the variety of the colours, bright or pastel, from deep red to indigo and mauve, depending on the hour of the day and the light.

The Olga Mountains (1,000 metres in altitude) consist of a small chain of rounded domes, like the shells of huge tortoises set in the sand. Scattered beads of an oversized necklace of red sandstone, they are the remains of the primary massif erected on the original substratum, broken up, then raised up by tectonic activity. Attacked by wind erosion, having been buffeted by sand swirling in the wind for thousands of years, they remain sacred for the Aborigenes, who consider them to be the mythological support of the Earth-mother, and call them "Katajuta" (mountains with several heads).

Ayer's Rock, which bears the name of the man who discovered it in 1873, is, at a distance of some thirty kilometres from there, the most famous of the "Inselbergs", "mountain-islands", which lie majestically dotted about on the desolate plain. Like a sleeping elephant, Ayer's Rock is the largest monolith in the world. It is 850 m. long, 340 m. high, and its 10-kilometre circumference is encircled by the track from Alice Springs, 400 kilometres away, as if by the loop of a lasso. Erosion has hollowed out a series of little channels, reminding one in places of the convolutions of the cerebrum, so that it has been nicknamed "the brain". The natives have decorated the vertical walls with rock drawings. It is by aeroplane that one can best discover it, and the view is superb, especially when the setting sun lights up the red sandstone with enchanting fairy lights.

In opposition to the central desert, the Australian coasts offer other magnificent landscapes.

Australia. Great contrasts and bizarre shapes: the Pinnacles (above), in the national park of Nambung, and the luxuriant vegetation of the Blue Mountains (left). The Olga Hills, near Alice-Springs (right).

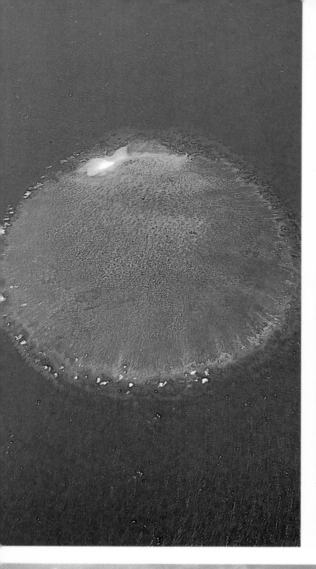

The hinterland behind Sydney is bordered by a range of hills, somewhat pompously called a "cordillera", in spite of its very modest height (1,200 metres). In fact, the "Blue Mountains" constitute a considerable obstacle and make penetration into the interior of the country very difficult. A jagged barrier of blue sandstone, 500 kilometres long and 80 wide, it can offer some fascinating views over the countryside. The cliffs of Port Campbell are the result of the unequal struggle between the sandstone coastline and the fury of the southern ocean. Wild and crumbling, the coast sees a few metres nibbled away each year, leaving behind pillars, arches and needle-like points, the usual results of this kind of battle.

More original is the north coast of Kimberley, mountainous, indented and lonely. Around Yampi Sound, with hollowed out bays and dotted with islands, illuminated by a rich fringe of coral, it conceals delightful emerald-green or opal-coloured lagoons, a charming reminder of enchanting Polynesia, voluptuously stretching out its coral atolls from the other side of the ocean.

Above and left : the Great Barrier Reef seen from an amazing angle (Australia) and two views of the cliffs at Port Campbell : the "Rocks of the Twelve Apostles". Right, top and opposite : the Milford Sound Falls and Lake Tekapo, in New Zealand.

NEW ZEALAND

Lost between Australia and Antarctica, the two adjacent islands that make up New Zealand are the most southerly inhabited region in the world apart from Adelie Land.

South Island, which is very mountainous, is dominated by the grim, forbidding aspect of the New Zealand Alps, culminating in the highest summit, Mount Cook (3,765 metres). Heavy but dignified, this imposing peak is situated in the middle of the spine of the island, and offers its most spectacular landscape.

At the end of South Island, the magnificence of the coasts, idented with "sounds" or "fjords", justifiably attracts a moderate influx of tourists, tourism being an economic factor which is gradually, though with difficulty, being developed here. Those who do make the visit can take advantage of the outstanding feeling of wildness and grandiose intensity of these still unspoilt surroundings. Milford Sound is indisputably the prime jewel of the collection, discovered at the end of the 19th century by Sutherland, a sealcatcher. It is a perfect glacial valley, into which the sea rushed over a distance of several kilometres in the heart of perpetually frozen mountains. The precipi-

tations are so heavy there (6,000 mm per year!) that the water of the fjord, diluted by the abundant rainfall and the constant trickling of the rain-water, consists of fresh water on the surface. Waterfalls, therefore, are numerous, though the Sutherland Falls are unique. The wasteway of Lake Quill, overhanging in a narrow circle of high mountains, these falls are perhaps the most dramatic in the world, falling in three stages from a height of 600 metres down a sheer, barren cliff.

North Island, aptly called "the smoking island", is an island of volcanos and all that goes with them.

THE PARADISE OF INDONESIA AND MELANESIA

Indonesia, a strange insular world, attractive but little known and often inhospitable, scatters its 13,000 islands between Asia and Australia.

Sumatra, Java and Bali are the most accessible for tourists. "The land of volcanos", as Java is called, because it can boast 140 of them, is an open-air museum of vulcanism. In this region of smoking mounds, crusty craters, sulphur concretions and charred scoria, Krakatoa and Tengger vie with each other in importance and interest.

Krakatoa owes its reputation as a bloodthirsty monster to its terrifying eruption of 1883. This was the most powerful explosion on earth before the atom-bomb was dropped on Hiroshima. It was heard as far away as Australia, a distance of 2,000 kilometres, and was accompanied by a projection of lava and ashes to a height of more than 30 kilometres.

Scattered like dust in the heart of the Pacific between Indonesia and New Zealand, the islands that go to make up Melanesia take their name from its black-skinned inhabitants.

The common denominator of all these islands, famous or completely unknown, apart from the negritude of its inhabitants, is represented by a fringe of casually-swaying coconut palms, flexible in the face of the trade winds, and the girdle of a shimmering lagoon.

Everybody knows New Guinea, the inhospitable Papua, wild and almost inaccessible. Under its new name, Vanuatu, the former New Hebrides, off all the main tourist routes, with its concealed, almost totally unspoilt landscapes, swept by frequent cyclones, has some of the most beautiful scenery in the Pacific.

Discovered by Cook in 1774, New Caledonia (so called because of its resemblance to Scotland) is a huge rock emerging from the sea.

Hub of the Central Pacific, the delightful islands of Viti Levu and Vanua Levu, go together to make up the attractive archipelago of Fiji. Within the effective protection of a barrier reef of coral, a magnificent lagoon, coloured with the subtle shades of a watercolour, laps gently against the interminable stretches of white sand, against a background of coconut palms.

BALI

The smallest of all the islands of Indonesia, and the first of the beads in the rosary of the Sunda islands, hanging like the tail of a kite being pulled along by Java. These geographical definitions unfortunately do not convey an idea of the true character of Bali. Territorially very small (120 kilometres by 70 kilometres) it is the heart and the smile of the Indonesian world, its legend and its international shop-window.

With its asymmetrical relief, centred on the cone of Mount Agung (3,140 metres), a formidable volcano whose last eruption took place in 1963 and devasted part of the island, Bali offers two very different faces; in the north, a dry coast, sparsely populated, protected from the monsoon, and made up of cliffs falling steeply down into the Java Sea; in the south, long beautiful beaches lie at the foot of well-watered, fertile slopes, covered with tropical plants. It is there that the temples and villages are to be found in a fairylike setting of humid vegetation, over which reign fabulous exotic orchids. Yet the Balinese landscape, the aestheticism of which is captivating in its strangeness, was, in fact, made by

man; the soul of it is the terraces; clustered together, they chisel and work away, they transform the land, climbing even the slightest slope, making it, of course, suitable for growing crops of some kind, but also adding a touch of magic which converts the hills into a vast stratified geometrical puzzle, recalling the oversized steps of an imaginary temple, occupying the whole mountain and climbing to conquer mist-capped peaks, in search of some invisible god. Carefully and lovingly tended, usually irrigated and impregnated by the multitude of springs which flow down from the summits, they are given up to growing rice. The extraordinary sight of these hanging rice-fields, real "water staircases", sparkling in the sunshine, is an experience of fascinating and unreal splendour.

The world of the tourists lies in the palaces that

line the heavenly beaches like Sanur Beach. From there, between two performances of ritual dances where the famous dancing girls with smooth, hieratic movements, mime the legend of Ramajans, magnificent excursions lead them to Lake Batur and Lake Bratan. In formidable, wild surroundings, certain villages, accessible only by boat, have preserved the Mazdean funeral rites of emaciation, as performed in India or Iran. Along the northern shore the temples, perched on the steep slopes, or hollowed out of the cliff, like the Pura-Luhur, offer them other superb "postcard" views. Unless they choose, as they climb the slopes of the Agung, to go through the area of the rice-fields, or the terraces planted with maize, manioc or clove-trees, to visit the temple of Basakih, the most sacred on the island.

It must be said, indeed, that everything is ideally combined; the active vulcanism is an expression of divine force, at the same time as a manifestation of the mysteries of nature.

Enchanting Bali. On these pages : the rice-plantations and the site of a sanctuary.

LAKE MASHU,
THE BAY OF MATSHUSHIMA,
MOUNT FUJI-SAN

The Japanese archipelago is rich in striking landscapes. The advanced crumbling state of the emerging land, and the abundance of volcanos of all kinds give the courtryside a mountainous, tormented look, and are the reason for its amazing diversity.

The volcanic island of Hokkaïdo, the furthest north, is an outstanding example: hollowed out into craters filled with superb incredibly limpid lakes, it can offer breathtaking panoramas, whose romantic charms must not make one forget the tremendous telluric forces that they conceal. Lake Mashu, with its restful pastel shades, fills with the most transparent of blue waters the caldera of an ancient volcano, from which emerges a last pustule of lava. The sight of this solitary lake, evanescent and sterile, where nothing can live, is an experience not to be missed.

To the south of Hokkaïdo, the enormous crater (2 kilometres in circumference) of Jigokudani, the infernal mouth, with sulphurous emanations and aggressive colours, provides a striking contrast with Mashu-Ko, and offers another aspect, harsher and more hostile, of the ever-present Japanese vulcanism.

Fortunately, the bay of Matshushima, on the east coast of the island of Hondo, offers soothing yet dazzling postcard views where a multitude of little islands, sculpted by erosion ans scalloped with light-couloured rocks, worn into cliffs and covered with a delicate mane of slender conifers, make' up the subject of a stylized, polished print; the bay is much praised by poets and very popular with tourists from all over the world.

One of the most famous sights in Japan, Mount Fuji is, without doubt, the best-known volcano in the world, just as its highest point (at 3,775 metres) is its symbol and its sacred summit. "Lotus flower with eight petals", that is how the Japanese with their enthusiasm and imagination see the summit of Mount Fuji, remarkable for its purity and harmony. Under a diaphanous cap of everlasting snow, its perfect cone rises in the bright azure sky like a mystical elevation. Faced with such a restful type of beauty, one feels far removed from the enormous geological upheavals that the frozen aestheticism of such perfect purity conceals: the 830 km^2 of the present mountain cover an older volcano, while numerous accessory craters open in its flanks, confirming that the giant is simply slumbering; its

topmost caldera, alive with fiumeroles and jets of
steam, is a reminder that the last eruption dates back
only to 1707, less than three centuries ago, which in
the life of a volcano is merely a short break.

Japan. Left, top : a cherry-tree in blossom in
front of the snowcovered cone of the famous
volcano Fuji. Below and above : peace and
harmony in this picture of the lake of Miyajima,
in the region of Hiroshima, an ideal spot for a
temple. Right : pretty little creeks, near
Matsushima.

THE BAY OF ALONG, KOREA

It is not only in China that the Far East can offer spectacular sights. It can offer a great many others outside China which are of the very first order. Among them, in Korea, "the land of the calm morning", there is the amazing viewpoint of To Dam Bong, where the vast estuary of the river Han, surrounded by a fringe of mountains of the delicate pastel shade of jade, and bristling with the "three peaks of Todam", very like one of the scenes to be seen on ancient pieces of china. And then there is the famous bay of Along, opening into the gulf of Tonkin, facing delta of Song Koï. Resulting from the collapse of a coastal range worn away by the waves, this represents a particularly spectacular episode in the battle between the sea and the limestone cliffs. Here, accelerated by the tropical climate, the process is at its peak, and the last sight of this crumbly archipelago is an extraordinary experience. It recalls the fantastic architecture of some dead village swallowed up by the waves; or some magnificent mountain debris that has run aground in the fishy shallows, no deeper than 20 metres. According to Vietnamese mythology, the unique landscape of this scattering of rocky islands rising

from the azure-blue waters of a small inland sea, "Lu Hai" (blue water), is the supernatural work of the Dragon, the all-powerful spirit of the waters. Ha Long, which means "where the dragon comes down" has been corrupted by westerners, into "Along".

When in the 17th century the Dutch sailor Hendrick was shipwrecked on the shores of this mysterious and unknown peninsula, he never suspected that he would spend five years there, before returning to Europe to disclose the secret of the remarkable beauties of the "Land of the Still Morning".

This "hermit state", so long forgotten, hidden in a cluster of mountains, which the monsoon in a generous mood covers with luxuriant forests, represents the ultimate refuge of an original culture and Asiatic traditions dating from thousands of years ago.

The multitude of temples, pagodas, tombs and cave sanctuaries which stand dotted about on the mountainside, scattered in the valleys, or perched high on the peaks of wooded ridges, erected there by those of the Buddhist faith, harmonise so perfectly with the countryside that one might almost believe them to have been brought about by some geological fantasy, rather than being the result of man's

These landscapes in Korea consist essentially of vegetation. The orchestral conductors of the natura-

listic symphony are the harshness of the continental
climate, which produces the extremely luminous
crystalline winters, and the effects of the monsoon,
the sap of the forests and the gardens, spreading
along the yellow strip of the sea-shore multicoloured
and sweet-smelling clusters of flowers and fruitful
orchards. Thus, camelias, magnolias and the blossom
of fruit trees are the essential ingredients of the most
ordinary of spring-time engravings.

When the smooth, pastel-shaded waters of a river
are combined with all this, they form an extraordinary scene, vapourous and evanescent, bathed in
poetry and dreams, steeped in unreal tones of jade or
porcelain. The grandiose setting of To-Dam-Sam-
Bong is the most perfect example of these subtle
harmonies, a constant reminder of the finest of
paintings on silk.

**Left : the Ahnap-Ji at Kyong-Ju, and the
grounds of a palace, at Seoul. Above : the
fairylike spectacle of the famous bay of Along
in Vietnam. Opposite : dusk on the Mekong,
in Laos.**

THE CHANSI LOESS, THE YANGTSI-KIANG, THE LANDSCAPES OF KOUEILIN

Between Mongolia and central China, the plateau of Chansi covers a territory as large as France with a thick layer of loess. Brought there by the wind from the Gobi deserts, this deposit of muddy sand has spread over everything, sometimes reaching a depth of 500 metres. Lacking any stratified structure, and perforated, in fact, by a great many tiny vertical channels, this loose covering of yellow earth is very crumbly and breaks up as it is eroded by the wind and the infiltration of the flowing water. The result is an amazing landscape of canyons separating a series of rising terraces, very small and anarchical, but fertile and lovingly cultivated.

It is in this land of the "yellow earth" that the Houang-Ho, the second largest river in China, has hollowed out its bed. The yellowish mud dissolves in its waters, colouring them deeply, and earning the river the nickname of "the yellow river".

The majestic course of the Yangtsi-Kiang (or Tchang-Kiang), the longest and most beautiful river in the country, serves as its symbol as well as its umbilical cord. It has some exceptional panoramas to offer. Created at an altitude of 4.600 metres, in the remote convulsions of Tibet, very near Mekong, another of the Asian giants, called in the high valleys "Mour Oussou", which means in Tibetan "winding water", it remains parallel to its neighbour at first, until it reaches the borders of the Indochinese

peninsular. But after Likiang, it chooses to make its way towards the distant China Sea. Thus, turning at an angle of 90°, it passes through a spectacular

China. Above : typical Kueilin countryside. Left : an effect of mist on the majestic Yang-Tse-Kiang. Below : the superb banks of the famous river, in the Kueilin.

succession of gorges, which make the journey downstream, between Tchoung King and Wouhan, the most picturesque boat trip that one can take anywhere in China. There are on this stretch of the river more than 100 kilometres of narrows and rapids, offering a grandiose vista, its magnificence increased even further by the hedge of sharp peaks that looks down over the gorges and the perfectly limpid waters, surprisingly free of the mud of other Chinese rivers, a fact that justifies its nickname of "the blue river". As it flows on its 2,000-kilometre course it finds in its path, in the heart of Seutchouan, the formidable obstacle of the Wouchans, an imposing massif, with about a dozen summits reaching a height of 3,000 metres or more.

Magnificent in its powerful force, the impetuous river throws itself into battle against the mountain and eventually manages to force its way through and cut the series of the three gorges of Yitchang. The most scenic, the Wu gorge, twists its way in rugged bends around the high walls which restrict it to a narrow passage over a distance of more than 40 kilometres.

The basin of Koueilin (or Guilin), only recently opened to foreign tourists, offers the most marvellous stretches of countryside in traditional China: the land of painters and poets, of evanescent dreams, carried out in pastel shades on the plates and screens of imperial art. The master behind this amazingly poetic creation, captivating and like something out of another age, is the erosion of the greatest karstic base in the world. Over a distance of 50 kilometres between Koueilin and Yangchouo, with its unpredictable fantasies the river Li constantly changes course

as it winds its way between the rocky spurs with their fantastic shapes. It could be the backcloth of a Peking opera or the decoration on a fan. Geology has created over the passing centuries a subtle composition of mad impressions that one is delighted to discover as one glides down on the still water. This exquisite emerald-green mirror reflects a petrified forest of sculpted stones, incredible spurs with their starkness softened by creeper and tropical vegetation.

One never tires of looking at the everchanging but ever-repeated aspects of the Kueilin (left). Above and opposite : the Likiang and the Li.

THE EVEREST MASSIF
THE VALLEY OF ANNAPURNA
KASHMIR AND KARAKORAM

An enormous mountain range, curving round in an arc between India and Tibet, over a length of 2,700 kilometres and a width of 250 milometres, the Himalayas extend through these countries, demarcating a multitude of river basins, valleys and massifs. The different parts of the range can boast a great variety in their flora and in their climate, though they all have in common the torrential rain of the monsoon season.

The Himalayas are mountains in the superlative. Everything there is huge and disproportionate to what we are accustomed to with other mountains: the peaks are the most fabulous, the mountain faces reach the most dizzy heights and are the most breathtakingly sheer, the glaciers are the most gigantic, the valleys the most grandiose. But in this concentration of spectacular landscapes and extraordinary sights, there are, nevertheless, certain regions that are especially remarkable as far as icy, inhuman and terrifying beauty is concerned.

It is because of its amazing 8,847 metres that Mount Everest has been given the nickname of "roof of the world". The indigenous population call it, more poetically, Chomolungma, "goddess, mother of the snows", for it was to be expected that the highest mountain massif in the world would be considered by the people who live at its foot as the dwelling-place of the gods, and the setting for many legends. The long trails of frozen snow, snatched up by the terrifying winds that buffet it continuously and make its almost unreal summit seem to be steaming as the snow is blown about, bear witness to its sovereign majesty. It reigns over a universe of glaciers on summits that are slightly lower, but whose silhouettes outlined on the sky are nonetheless superb. In the shadow of the giant, Mount Ehotse, with its long elevated crests, the perfect pyramid of Mount Makalu, the elegant Pumori and, further east, the powerfully impressive Kangchenjunga (8,600 metres high) treasure-house of eternal snow and the moun-

tain held sacred by sherpas, making up, high above Nepal, the most outstanding mountain panorama in the world.

But Everest eclipses them all by the fascination it holds and has held since last century when an undistinguished little British official, whose name it bears, measured it and proclaimed it to be the highest point on our planet. Since then expeditions have succeeded each other on its ice-covered faces, with a history of tragedies and successes, from the disappearance of Mallory and Irving in 1924 until the victory of Hillary and Sherpa Tensing in 1953. The high valley, given over to the monastery of Rongbuk, in Chinese Tibet, into which entry is now forbidden, provides a spectacular approach route to this royal peak, which appeared to Mallory, who sang its praises but also died for it, as "the amazing white tooth set in the jaw of the world".

The first "8000" to be conquered, by French climbers in 1950, Mount Annapurna stands dominating a massive range, elegant and remote, which stretches from Mount Dhaulagiri (8,172) to Mount Manaslu (8,156), other great lords of the land. The steepness of its slopes, its lofty ridges, the beauty of its glacial valleys and its falling torrents, make it a marvellous area for alpinists, at the same time as

Above : a view of the massif of Everest, the "roof of the world" (height : 8 847 metres), in Nepal. Right : the Annapurna (its highest point stands at 8 078 metres) and the glaciers of the Karakoram (Pakistan).

being one of the most attractive regions of the Himalayas, spotted from afar by means of the haughty characteristic outline of Mount Macchapuchare (6,997), one of the "golden lotus petals" created by Vishnu.

Kashmir, its name as soft and gentle as the caress of a cashmere shawl, offers the traveller everything to seduce him and a whole range of different landscapes. Starting from the enchantment of the lakes of the "blessed valley" of Srinagan, one plunges straight into the formidable complex mountain mass of the Karakoram, meaning in Turkish "black scree". The harshness, the ruggedness, the barrenness and the bare stone of this gigantic conglomeration of mountains is both breathtaking and frightening. This is especially true of the terrifying Nanga Parbat (8,126 metres), in Sanskrit "bare mountain", the giant mountain that has claimed more victims than any other in the Himalayas, and the mountain that legend holds to be populated by evil spirits. Thirty climbers were killed on its slopes before it allowed itself to be climbed in 1958. And there is also K.2, or Chogori, the second highest mountain in the world (8,611 metres) its pyramid standing like an overpowering sentinel, untouched and unclimbed until

1951. This is the area in which the most extensive glaciers in the world are to be found; half a dozen of them are longer than 50 kilometres, and are famous for their exceptionally high rate of growth, sometimes reaching as much as five metres' progression in an hour.

Baltoro is the most beautiful of all. Its petrified valley, bristling with sparkling seracs, opalescent and transparent, and blue-green in colour, is framed by a magnificent surrounding hedge of icy peaks over 7,000 metres high.

Amongst all these giants of oustanding beauty, the prize for charm and elegance must go to the elegant Nanda Devi. Less high (7,127), but composed in perfect harmony, it casts between its twin peaks a delicate ridge of snow, unreal in the intensity of its whiteness, which is considered to be the "pearl of the Himalayas".

Above : at a height of 3 500 metres, at the foot of the Nanga Parbat, the "bare mountain" (Pakistan). Below : a view of the famous valley of Katmandou. Right : a landscape in Kashmir, in India.

THE VALLEY OF BAMIYAN, THE BANDI AMIR LAKES

The complex massif of Hindoukouch serves as the backbone of Afghanistan. A threatening range of mountains, formed by earthquakes, it acts as a formidable barrier. The eastern part of the range, which joins up with the Himalayas and reaches a height of over 7,000 metres, is not very well known and very difficult to reach. The western end, however, more open and accessible, contains vast stores of marble and, more important still, of lapis lazuli, which have been exploited since the days of antiquity. Within the shelter of its southern buttresses, huddle the two best-known tourist spots of Afghanistan.

The valley of Bamiyan appears to the traveller like a refuge, oasis of peace and serenity, in a difficult, even hostile, region. At one time, this peaceful charm was able to attract merchants and travellers, who willingly tarried there, to such an extent that it became a meeting-place for discussion and meditation. Between the 1st and 3rd centuries, monasteries were hollowed out of the rocks, as well as the alveoles containing the famous giant statues of Buddha; and the mystical prestige of the valley was to last long after the Islamization of the country. The most important thing here is not the village, bound within its girdle of sand castles, nor the picturesque bazaar, perfumed with the smell of spices and incense. It is rather the overall view of the setting that you can admire by climbing the hill from which the ruins of the old citadel dominate the village. The soft refined setting of this little valley preserves and draws from it all the attraction of its great majetic beauty.

At a distance of 80 kilometres from there, the most moving experience of your journey through Afghanistan awaits you, with the beautiful sight of a string of lakes, the Bandi Amir lakes, which stretch like a necklace of pearls, set into the gangue of the cretaceous plateau. An unforgettable sight, a jewel of mineral perfection, of which visitors to the region are unanimous in their praise, as they vie with each other in their extravagant descriptions in honour of one of the most wonderful landscapes on earth. The walk up the interminable approach, along a dusty, monotonous track, in rocky surroundings, desolate and torrid, under the frowning gaze of a haughtily hostile Hindoukouch, are ideal preliminaries for the unexpected discovery of these fabulous stretches of water, heightened by the contrast. Imagine five hanging lakes, jewels laid in the treasure-chest of the surrounding rocks, separated by little natural dams and intervening stretches where a network of canals water charming amphibious gardens with luxuriant vegetation so unexpected in this context.

For, what explains the stunned admiration of the visitor is the geometrical exactness, the perfection of these natural masterpieces; the proportions are perfect; the limpidity of the water is unbelievable; the sparkle of the opalescent surface, sometimes turquoise, sometimes emerald green or lapis lazuli in colour, is breathtaking in its purity. It needs even the most sensory series of sunrises and sunsets, the variety of the intermediate canals supplying their personal garden, to humanize a little such a perfect jewel, almost too pure to move the visitor and to arouse in him anything but enthusiastic admiration.

Afghanistan. Left, top and right : the lakes of Band-i-Amir, like precious stones in the desert. Opposite : the massif of Hindoukouch.

MOUNT ARARAT AND LAKE VAN, THE ELBROUZ AND THE DEMAVEND MASSIFS, THE LOUT DESERT

An enormous pyramid, perpetually covered with snow, at the meeting-point of the present frontiers between Turkey, the U.S.S.R. and Iran, Mount Ararat is a mythological, historical and religious mile-stone, as much as a mountain. Reaching a height of 5,465 metres at its highest point, its summit is revered in the Judeo-Christian tradition for having been the landing place of Noah's ark, loaded with all the animals in creation that had been rescued from the water, at the end of the great flood mentioned in the Bible. These same waters, whose disasters were to be found well before the Old Testament in Babylonian writings, seem to be a sign of cataclysmic rainfall and terrible floods, of which archaeological research has found traces on all the sites in Mesopotamia during the 4th millenary before Christ.

It was first climbed in 1829, but enthusiastic climbers continue to look under the ice of the summit for remains of the Ark, still bringing back from time to time, even after thousands of years, amazing timber beams, for example, perfectly preserved...

It is towards the little Turkish town of Dogubayazit that this superb mountain turns its best profile.

Not far from here, the picturesque hollow containing Lake Van, well away from the main roads, offers the magnificent landscapes, mountainous, wild and desolate of the old Armenia. The Elbrouz is a formidable range of mountains, set around the Caspian Sea. In the north, it reaches up to the Caucasus, while its southeren end separates the dry and torrid central Iranian plateau from the muggy, humid shores of the Caspian Sea. And what a contrast it makes, this massif of Alpine type, perpetually covered with snow, rising up like some unusual kind of defensive wall above the desert-like steppe surrounding Teheran and serving as a piedmont for the town. The rare valleys cutting their way through this rugged mass, are reached by aerial, almost acrobatic routes, leading to vast and splendid landscapes. The most scenic of all is that which takes in the characteristic pyramid of the Demavend. Reaching more than 5,600 metres in height, this extinct volcano, its peak everlastingly capped with ice and its crater perpetually frozen over, is not without a certain charm of its own. It looks rather like a more elegant, more slender Mount Ararat.

Like all outstanding peaks, this mountain has a mystical vocation, the old eastern mythologies having made it the dwelling-place of Gilgamesh, the legendary hero of Persia and Ancient Mesopotamia.

The centre of Iran, embraced by a high mountainous belt which runs round the borders of the country, lies in a vast depression, which at the time of the prehistoric period was covered by the sea, and later became an immense desert presenting several different aspects. In the north, the "Kevir", very stony ground, which is the equivalent of the "Reg" in the Saharan area, is crossed by monotonous tracks and very sparsely populated in the few villages they run through. To the south, the "Lout", a mineral desert, total desert, unlike any other in the world.

Without either animal or vegetable life, where a permanent diabolical wind cuts into strange rocky forms, the "Kaluts", long banks of rock of more than a hundred kilometres by sixty, and eighty metres in height, these stony spurs separate the rolling dust-blown dunes, the "Rigs", corresponding to the "Ergs" in the Sahara. As the whole desert is completely inaccessible, one has to content oneself, between Kerman, Bam and Zahedan, with admiring the overpowering barren deserted mountains which rise up on its borders. Their tawny colour, turning to mauve, pink or purple, according to the light at the time, provide a unique spectacle which is at the root of the incomparable fascination of these oppressive lands, lost and seemingly abandoned at the end of the world.

As one stands here, one can imagine that one is at the dawn of creation, when only the mineral world existed on our planet.

Left: a view of the chain of the Elbrouz, in Iran. Below: the highest mountain in the country, north-east of Tehran, Mount Demavend. Right: a green plain at the foot of the enormous snowy pyramid of Mount Ararat (Turkey).

PLACES OF INTEREST IN THE SAHARA
DJERID SOUR, M'SAB AND THE HOGGAR

A vast arid expanse, between North Africa and Black Africa, covering nine million square kilometres, the Sahara is the largest desert in the world. But especially the most beautiful and the most varied. The centre is taken up by a mass of high rugged rocks, laid bare through erosion: Adrar, Air, Hoggar, Lassili and Tibesti. the "ergs", an infinite stretch of rolling dunes surrounds them, sheltering in their deep and hidden folds wonderful oases which are a reminder that the Sahara has not always been a desert.

In prehistorical times, there existed on this deso-late land, a vast hydrographic network, allowing hunters to survive, in dense, abundant vegetation, as is borne out by the fossilized forests exposed by the wind. Nothing is left of this today: only total desert, which is gradually losing its last caravans of camel-drivers, although it was a common sight to see them still crossing the desert from one oasis to another, during last century.

The southern part of Tunisia offers the magnificent palm-groves of Tozen and Nelta, the latter clustered together in the hollowed-out depression, sparkling with springs, of the famous "Basket".

The Djerid proudly displays its "chotts", the bottom of salty hollows, their sparkling white crusts cracking under the burning rays of the sun. The Souf symbolizes the evanescent, unreal charm of the great Eastern Erg, the realm of mirages. Here the sand and the dunes reign alone; and man must everywhere submit to their all-powerful domination. Touggourt, the starting-point for the "Black Cruise" of Citroën, and especially El Oued are its brightest jewels. The fellaheen empirically find proof of the existence of underground streams, by means of a type of palm-grove, a unique kind of garden: the sand is hollowed out into huge funnel-shaped holes right down to the point where they reach the dampness of the deeply-buried water-bearing bed, which feeds the central well supply.

The Sahara. The centre of this immense desert is occupied by the rocky hills of the Tassili (above) and the Hoggar (bottom, left). Between the two : the palm-groves of Skoura, in the Valley of the Dades, in Morocco. Right : the oasis of Djamet, in the massif of the Tassili (top) and the oasis of Elquatta, in Algeria (below).

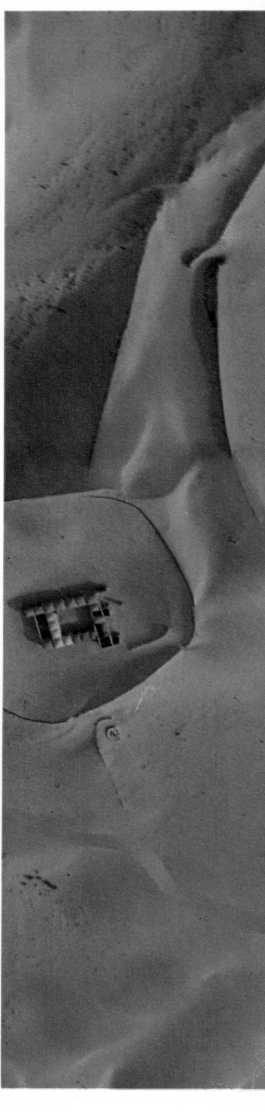

But the most spectacular of the Saharan landscapes awaits you elsewhere, in the heart of the rocky massifs where wind erosion has, over a period of thousands of years, sculpted strange, even fantastic, shapes in surrealistic style.

The Hoggar, a crystalline substratum as large as the whole of France, reshaped in the Tertiary by a volcanic upheaval, is the best known and the most accessible secret redoubt in the desert. A real water castle of the Sahara, from which spring a number of undeveloped wadis, which run down to disappear in the sea of sand encircling the rocks, forming there the precious "gueltas", providential pools or water-holes, a blessing for travellers. It is a harsh, inhospitable region, with still a few Touareg occasionally to be found there. It was the legendary home of Foucault's father and General Laperrine. Brought into fashion by Frison Roche, climbers found there a new territory for their sport, technically very difficult, and having the advantage of an exceptional environment.

The massif of the Assekrem, with a high peak reaching more than 3,000 metres, towers over this mineral world, hostile and petrified, surrounded by the yellowish fringe of the Erg, making the heat-haze of its mirages hover over the horizon.

Above : the Great Western Erg, near Tagbit. Below : a small oasis of the Great Eastern Erg, near Touggourt. Right : an aerial view of an oasis surrounded by the all-invading, all-powerful sand.

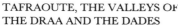

TAFRAOUTE, THE VALLEYS OF THE DRAA AND THE DADES

In the folds of the high Atlas mountains are hidden the most beautiful stretches of countryside in Morocco.

Beyond its piedmont begins what is called "the great south" which rouses one's imagination and consists of all that is fascinating in the most majestic and imposing pre-Saharan panoramas of the "Maghreb", a word which means "setting" in Arabic.

The Tizi N'Tienka and the Tizi N'Tes passes cross the impressive barrier of the Atlas mountains at an altitude of 2,500 metres, opening the door to this much-coveted universe. One feels oneself to be in another world, wherever one goes, as much in all that concerns the country itself, as in Ehab and the men closely linked with it, and perfectly integrated there. The charming little suspended valley of Tafraoute is pure delight. It can be reached from Tiznit, by means of a road which climbs up through the mountainous basins, tawny in colour and very arid, stifling in the heat in summer. The short valley of Tafraoute is perched on the flank of the Atlas mountains, in a cirque of pink granite. The land of the Ammelns, a tribe of Chleuhs, sedentary and hard-working, it is perfectly exposed to full advantage: the delicate green of the cereals and the sweet-smelling blossoming orchards, as white as snow, adding their splash of brightness to the chaotic pink of the rocks, where Ksom and Kaslos are scattered, in perfect harmony with the mineral enclosure that surrounds them.

Draa, Dades, Todra and Ziz, bear the fine-sounding names of humble little wadis, almost non-existent or torrent-like, according to the will of the seasons, but all flowing down from the high central Atlas mountains. From Ouarzazate the Draa runs directly towards the south, winding its ways through the irregularities of a piedmont which is deserted, wind-swept and desolate. A string of rustling palm-groves, in the shade of which nestle orchards and gardens, is stretched out all along the river, under the protection, now useless, of Ksour, much diminished but still superb.

The wali Dades is even more spectacular. Because it has the greatest difficulty in freeing itself from the grip of the Atlas range, it has to cut itself a high breach, measuring 300 metres, in stark, inhuman vertical rock faces, where only the midday sun manages to reach right down to the bottom. It thus has the power to escape from its mineral prison on a bed of pebbles. To compensate for the harshness of this part of its course, the place where it joins up with the Draa is a real sight to delight the eye. There it is that the most beautiful oases are to be found. (They used to serve as stopping places for the caravans making their way up from the nearby desert.) There too the crenelated walls of the citadels in reddish mud in all their warmth of colour, sucked dry and gradually worn away like sand-castles, are the most imposing and the most proud and dignified; there too that each village looks like the setting prepared for the acting out of a scene from the adventures of Marco Polo, for this kind of architecture is amazingly similar to the medieval buildings of the Yemen and the Near East. The burning heat of the sun, the yellow powder of the sand-storms, coming in torrid blasts from the invisible desert, omnipresent, add to the oppressive but fascinating atmosphere of the great south.

Morocco. This page : the valleys of the Todra, Tafraout and, bottom, of Lourika. Right : the great oasis of Bumah, on the banks of the river Dades. Below : view of a mountain massif of the High Atlas mountains.

LAKE KIVU AND LAKE TANGANYIKA, THE KALAMBO FALLS

Occupying the bottom of a western branch of the "Rift Valley", tectonic rift that crosses Africa from the Red Sea, Lake Kivu is in the centre of one of the most beautiful of all African landscapes. Its trough, formed a thousand million years ago, is startlingly spectacular because of its very indented shoreline and the outline of volcanic mountains which rise from the edge of it. A dense forest and luxuriant vegetation, nourished by the abundance of the equatorial rainfall, add to the splendour of the setting. At an altitude of 1,460 metres, its 2,600 km²

represent the highest concentration of water in this cicatricial fault in the crust of the earth. This superb stretch of blue water, festooned with greenery, is towered over by the solid overpowering mass of Mount Niragongo, one of the most famous volcanos in Africa, known through the explorations of H. Tazieff: its truncated cone (3,470 metres in height) used to contain a permanent lake of molten lava, marvellous but terrifying, but this has disappeared since the last eruption in 1976.

Next to Lake Kivu, in the same trough, Lake Tanganyika is much larger (650 kilometres long and from 30 to 80 kilometres wide, a total of 32,000 km²), but of a similar type: it is a trough lake, and has a

depth of more than 1,500 metres, appearing to be the prisoner of a mountainous yoke, with the harshness removed by waterfalls and volcanos, which make it one of the most beautiful panoramas to be seen on any lake in the world. Its great depth allows for a thermic stratification of its waters: the superficial layers are warm, very dark blue in colour and so limpid that an exceptional transparency is assured down to a depth of 15 metres. This is ideal for fishing.

At its northern end stand the range of the now no longer active Virunga volcanos, including Rumoka. Majestic and especially aesthetic, it possesses a crater 400 metres in diameter, creating an extraordinary impression. To the south, the Kalambo Falls, dropping in one single stream in a straight fall of 220 metres, are the most remarkable of all the waterfalls which cascade noisily down the rock-faces around the lake.

Left, top : the mountain massif of Kapsiki, in the north of the Cameroons. Above : a landscape of Mali. Left and below : the headland of Bukavu and the town of the same name, on Lake Kivu, in Zaire. Right : Rhumsiki Needle, in the Cameroons.

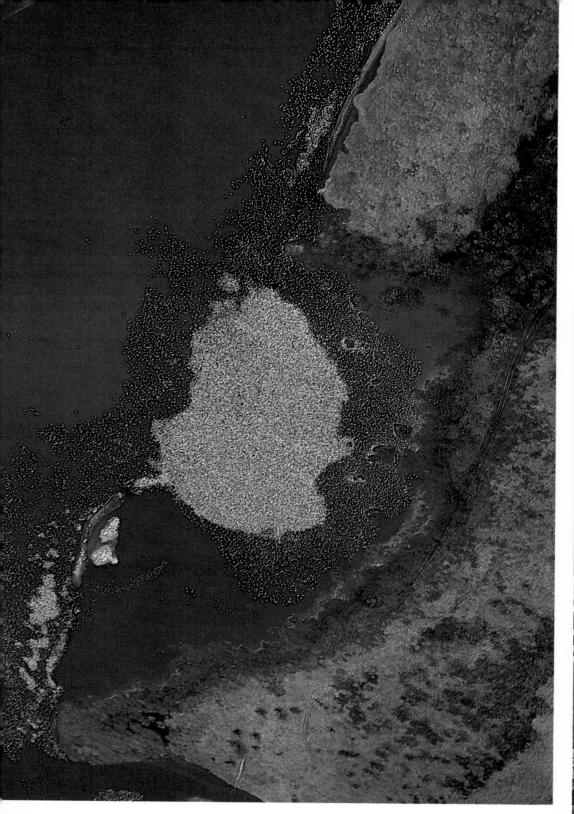

DANAKIL, THE VALLEY OF THE OMO, THE ENNEDI MASSIF

From the coast of the Somali to Mozambique, a deep tectonic fault runs through eastern Africa, influencing the special country that is to be found there, basically brackish lakes, salty deserts and volcanic mounds.

These views, which one might almost believe to be imaginary, are views of Central African landscapes : a lake in Kenya (left); below : the massif of the Ennedi, in Tchad. Below : formation in salt on the surface of a lake in Ethiopia (below the level of the sea).

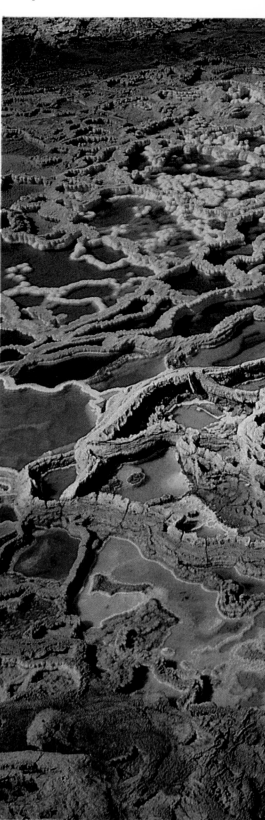

The vast desert-like plain of the Danakil is a depression set between the high plateaus of Eritrea, with, in the centre, a torrid, hostile desert, looking and feeling like the end of the world. This unbearable furnace is dominated by Mount Dallol, whose mere 38 metres make it seem really quite a mountain compared with the salty landscape surrounding it, at a height of 120 metres below the level of the Red Sea. Covered with pools of reddish briny water, this infernal depression is given up to still very primitive exploitation by the tribes known as the "salt-cutters". At 155 metres, Lake Assal, twice as salty as the Dead Sea, belongs to this same desolate world of extremes and excesses.

The point of the Danakil triangle is prolonged towards the south-east by the valley of the Omo, a group of strange salty lakes, joined by the rather haphazard, but beneficial course of the only spring of fresh water in the area, and encircled by diabolical

geological reliefs, the result of the vulcanism which orginally gave the edges of the fissure their shape.

The numerous lakes are for the most part nothing but superb stretches of blue-green water, so full of salt and alkali that their banks look like snow-covered land, sparkling and gleaming white, surrounded by vast plains of soda! Evaporation reaches more than 300 centimetres a year in this dried-up basin, cracked and steaming with caustic heat. There is virtually no life there.

To the south of the Sahara, the 60,000 km² of steep red sandstone slopes which make up the solid, imposing massif of the Ennedi, recall the sheer cliffs of the Tassili, in that the environment of this part of Tchad, the south-eastern corner, on the borders with the Sudan, is almost equally desert-like and desolate. Although the Ennedi is its water-tower in the form of a crumbling citadel, between pillars of granite looking like ruined crenelated towers, broad valleys,

today dried up, recall the ghosts of the generously full rivers which brought life to this desert in prehistoric times. Now nothing grows here but thorny chick-peas and stringy roses of Jericho.

Lake Tchad, geometrically at the heart of Africa, with uncertain contours, changing with the rhythm of the seasons, offers the surprise of an aquatic world lost in the middle of the desert. This great unusual stretch of blue water, fringed with marshy land and dotted with a myriad of little islands, is all that remains of the enormous inland sea which once used to fill the depression separating Tibesti from the Central African Republic.

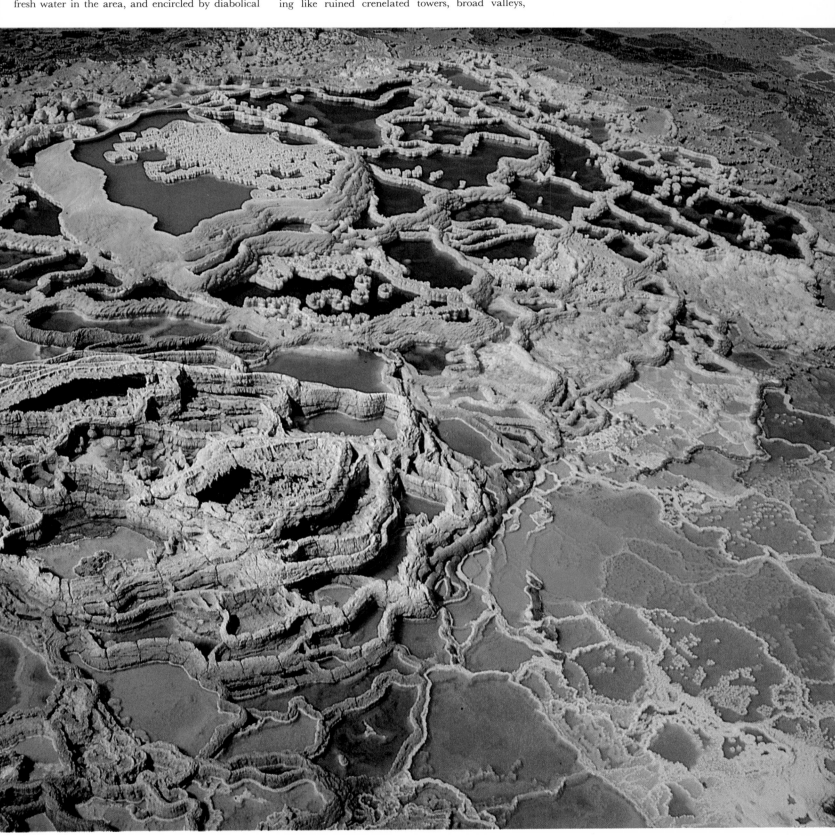

LAKES NATRON AND NAKURU, LAKE VICTORIA

The great geological fault in eastern Africa, which stretches out through Kenya, a real scar marking the ancient geological upheavals, gathers together the highest density of great natural landmarks on the whole of the African continent.

Mount Kenya, which has given its name to the country, dominates this region with its towering 5,200 metres, a region which abounds in telluric irregularities, a prolongation, in fact, of the Ethiopian "Rift Valley" beyond Lake Rudolph. The gentle slopes of the mountain, carpeted up to a very high level with a covering of green tropical vegetation, are crowned with an imposing jagged crest at the summit, where snow becomes perpetually incrusted and ice clings all the year round. The old crater has remained blocked by a column of viscous lava, cooled and petrified, which it never managed to discharge completely.

Of the Menengai (2,300 metres high) there is nothing left but a giantsized caldera of 80 km², the unpretentious, almost riduculous debris of the initial cone, long ago reduced to dust by a huge eruption. The bottom of the depression is riddled with a series of little lakes, alternating with cataracts and stretches of lava, which guarantees the variety and beauty of the unusual, rather strange countryside, because of the odd aggressive colours produced by the excessive mineralization of the water, and the specific microalgae which develop there. The multiplicity of these hollows where the water accumulates makes it the greatest natural reserve in Africa.

Lakes Natron and Magadi are particularly outstanding: their banks covered with festoons of crystallized soda in dazzling crusts look as if they are constantly covered with snow; while the accumulation of red algae in their bitter waters give them a bright scarlet colour.

The lofty cone of the volcano Ol Doinyo Lengai,
capped since 1966 with trickling lava, turned to an immaculate white through a chemical reaction, completes this unusual illusion of a wintry landscape. The contrast of millions of flamingoes, drawn there by the enormous concentrations of blue-green algae in Lake Nakuru, adds to the fairylike scene in this exceptional region, a paradise for birds and a mineral fresco painted in dazzling colours.

Between this and the range of the Mitumba mountains, lies another great reservoir of natural beauty, Lake Victoria, which owes its fame and its power to rouse imagination, to the mystery that surrounds it. An amazing inland sea (300 kilometres in diametre and 6,800 square kilometres in area) seemingly endless but shallow (an average of 50 metres), dotted with islands, and reflecting a sky in which the clouds often form to give a sign of good crops to come. Kampala and Entebbe have developed on its banks, making it the busiest lake in Africa. Discovered only in 1859, because of its situation well off the main routes by which the country was explored, its outlet is as famous as the lake itself, since it is the famous White Nile, the distant source of the great Nile.

Left : a curious arc formed by erosion, in Namibia, and rocks in the middle of the immense Lake Victoria, in Tanzania. Below : Lake Nakuru, in Kenya, very rich in algae and a paradise for birds. Right : a cascade in the tropical forest (Mount Kenya).

VICTORIA FALLS
THE KILIMANDJARO

On the way towards the Victoria Falls, the undisputed masterpiece of the natural wonders of the African continent, a detour to see the Lofoï Falls too is well worth while and will offer a pleasantly surprising sight. The sandstone bastion of Kundelungu, dominating the monotonous grassy plains of the Lufira, which stretch their savanna far and wide at an altitude of 800 metres, stands aloft, lonely and massive, ridged with a network of valleys cut out of the rock to allow an outlet for a number of secondary rivers. Plunging into this vertical-sided gorge, they are swallowed up in a thunderingly noisy whirlpool. The Lofoï is one of these streams; but its falls are the finest in the Kundelungu: one single cascade falls over 340 metres of sheer cliff, to disappear in a glorious spluttering spray.

However, they seem ridiculous beside the Victoria

Falls, a brutal accident in the peaceful Zambezi, which it swallows up in a frightening sound of thunder. They can be seen from more than 50 kilometres away because of the white cloud of spray that the rising air, released by the power of the falls, lifts 200 metres above the steppe.

Livingstone was the first man to see this breathtaking sight, on 16th November 1855: Over a width of 2 kilometres, the lazily-flowing Zambezi tumbles down into a telluric fault, more than 100 metres deep, which suddenly breaks up the undulating plateau through which it winds its way. In April, the time of the high waters, 6,000 m³ are thrown over the edge into space, with a deafening groan.

There are four stretches of cataracts to be distinguished, separated by the "islands" of the river: the small cataract "the Devil's Cataract", in the west, a mere 40 metres wide; the main falls, with their two "arms" of 500 metres and 300 metres: the "Rainbow", the widest with its 600 metres; and lastly, the

400 metres of the Eastern Cataract. All this goes to make up an incomparable sight, unique in the world, which can be admired from a network of paths and several belvederes. The most famous is "Danger Point", which well deserves its name, where one is torn, under the heavy rain of drops of spray, between admiration and fear. A bridge thrown over the narrow vertiginous zigzagging gorge which serves as a bubbling outlet for the split-up river, at a depth of 150 metres, adds, if this is possible, to the feeling of terrifying magnificence.

Only Mount Kilimandjaro (with an altitude of 5,895 metres), proud of its image and reputation, has preserved its haughty, distinguished shape, and reigns over the privileged world of the Massai tribes. The highest point in Africa, the best-known and the most famous mountain on this black continent, it proudly lines up its three volcanic cones, Shira, Mawenzi and Kibo. They are of the same type as the puys of Auvergne, with hollowed-out craters which, because of the altitude, become filled up with snow. Since the first ascent by Hans Meyer in 1889, however, the temperature has risen. Now the snow there melts and its place is taken by smoke from the fumeroles, proof that not all activity has ceased.

Top : two views of the famous Victoria Falls, in Zimbabwe. Left : a view of one of the lakes in the national park of Serengeti, in Tanzania. Right : the well-known silhouette of Mount Kilimandjaro.

THE AUGRABIES FALLS AND
THE CANYON OF THE GREAT FISH RIVER,
THE DRAKENSBERG MASSIF

Another southern country, South Africa, consists of a high plateau bordered with solid, massive mountains separating it from the coast, also very rocky and indented. Within the shelter of this mountain wall, the powerful river Orange, which has given its name to a province of the country, flows phlegmatically on

tres wide, at a height of only 600 metres, it constitutes the highlight of the immense depression of the great Koroo (400 kilomètres/120), which runs along the arid piedmont of the mountain that marks off the hinterland of Port Elisabeth. Strange, tormented mountainsides, where in total anarchy are dotted, peaks, chaos, eroded columns crests and flanks of ruiniform rocks, making up an unusual and inhospitable landscape. These festoons in stone, carved in the sandstone and the granite, give a lighter touch

its way towards the Atlantic. At a distance of 500 kilometres from its estuary, its majestic course must cross a fault measuring 146 metres, thus producing the Augrabies Falls. Higher than the Victoria Falls, though much less well known, they form a rocky amphitheatre in a semi-circular shape. Their particularity is that they thunder down into a vast cavity hollowed out at the foot of the cliff, which acts as a sounding board, a fact that explains the powerful roaring sound produced by the tumultuous waters, and justifies their name of "Hottentot of Aukurabis", "the waters that groan".

It is an affluent of the Orange, the Great Fish River, that is at the origin of one of the most desolate and inhospitable mineral scars that one could ever find. This arid, gloomy canyon, has an unimposing arrangement of its strata, its cornices and its furrowed rock-faces, making it look like an old dried-up wound, dark and horny, cutting through the surface of the tabular plateau, which is slightly softened by a gentle rustling of grass. One might think it was a geological scale model, without feeling and lifeless, if it were not for the reddish waters of a lost river flowing at the bottom of the mineral scar and the "Valley of Desolation", still with this same oppressive and pitiful atmosphere. A broad ravine, 300 me-

to a desert-like and moving setting, where drought reigns.

It is further to the north that the range of coastal mountains rises, broadens out and becomes a dominating massif, forming the framework of the province of Lesotho: the Drakensberg, "mountain of the dragon". There too one finds panoramas that are almost Alpine, with sharply pointed peaks, vertical rock-faces, gorges (the canyon of Blyde) or waterfalls like the Maletsunyane Falls, vaporous, falling like a broad ribbon from a height of 250 metres, watering with their spray the valley called by the natives "the land of smoke".

The impressive basalt summits (3,480 metres), swept by the frequent ocean gales, are dark clad and austere, giving this water-tower, from which flow all the rivers of the region, the air of a threatening fortress, defending the entrance to the basin of Kimberley, famous for its valuable diamond mines.

South Africa. Above : the impressive sight of the city of Cape Town, at the foot of Table Mountain. Right, top : the immense "amphitheatre" of the Drakensberg. Below : the Valley of Desolation. Right : the vineyards of the valley of Great Fish River.

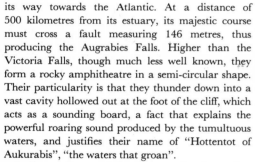